In God We Trust
Dollar$
& Sense

In God We Trust
Dollar$
& Sense

Debt is **NOT** your **Destiny!**
Money Management Principles for Success!

Frank Reed

Jon Clarke Publishing Group
www.jonclarkepublishing.com

In God We Trust: Dollars and Sense
ISBN 0-9761108-4-9
Copyright 2008 by Frank Reed

Cover Design by Rhonda Johnson (www.jonclarkepublishing.com)
Interior Design by Rhonda Johnson
Tina E. Clark

To the late Pastor James Shannon, who was a mentor, a friend and Pastor all rolled into one. He was an awesome teacher of God's word and he loved to preach the word of God. Because he believed in me, he gave me my very first start teaching about God's financial plan. He also taught me how to study the word of God and to savor the sweet nectar of God's word.

One of his favorite sayings about the word was: They are more precious than gold, than much pure gold; they are sweeter than honey, than honey from the comb. (Psalm 19:10)

Thank you Pastor Shannon I am eternally grateful.

Contents

Foreword

I met Frank Reed many years ago when we worked together on an article he wrote. After being out of touch for many years, he found me again and told me about his new project – a book that would help people use the Bible to steer their lives clear of debt. He asked if I would help him edit it and I straight out agreed. I hadn't been to church since I was a child and I wasn't at all familiar with the religious portion of this project. But Frank went to all that trouble to find me. That meant something and I was in.

I packed up the manuscript and hauled it to an island off the coast of Maine where I went through it page by page. One evening, rather exhausted, I looked up from my reading and there was a weathered sign over the door I had missed earlier. It read, "Trust in God." It was a clear indication for me that working with Frank on this project was the right thing to do. And many months later, when I finally finished, I could honestly say that through Frank and his book, I learned to appreciate his interpretation of what God had put before us in order to live an honest and debt-free life.

Debt remains an overwhelming problem for people throughout our communities. It's crushing individuals and families at record speed. Why aren't we able to get a grasp of this problem and solve it quicker? In God We Trust provides an obvious answer: follow the Bible correctly, truly live by the word and the rest will fall into place. Frank clearly discusses relevant passages of the Bible and explains how to use this information to make a positive impact on lowering personal debt. Through sharing his own personal accounts, Frank has written a book that is both entertaining and enlightening. It provides a well-defined plan for reducing debt using the words of the Bible to clearly draw a path to financial freedom. Frank's extensive knowledge of scripture, combined with his financial background, results in a book that shows us how to purposefully use God's word to bring us back to financial independence.

Chapter 1

The Game of Life

Every day we wake up to this journey called life. We get out of bed, our feet touch the floor, and the game begins. This is a race that most of the time we don't even realize we have entered. We just call it life!

What is this game called life? Who are the key players? And how did I get signed up in this game anyhow? These are questions that come to us after many years and after obtaining a lot of battle scars. We stop and think about it. What am I doing? How did I get here?

As a child, we have great dreams of becoming a doctor, lawyer, farmer, writer, homemaker, actor, professional athlete, etc. We spend most of our waking moments dreaming of the day, when? When I get older, I am going to be _____. You fill in the blank. We set out trying to find that elusive path to success. Ah, there is that word—success. The word we have all been searching for. We have been told that once we obtain it, then all of our dreams will come true!

What is success? Every day, people get up in the morning. Some struggle to find a state of consciousness, while others wake up excited about the expectation of the day. Both groups of people go through the same morning routine. They get dressed. They sit down at the table and eat breakfast or just grab a cup of coffee, then they reach for the car keys and off they go on their great quest to find success.

By the end of the day, these warriors return home. Some are already excited about tomorrow while others seem hopeless and depressed.

Here are two groups of people who started out on the same journey but found totally different results.

Most people don't know the real meaning of success. For too many Americans, success is having a large house, expensive cars, designer clothes, fine jewelry and a degree hanging on the wall. I don't believe there is anything necessarily wrong with having those things. But we need to understand that they are only the by–products of success. Isn't it possible that we are missing the true meaning of success?

I believe that the true meaning of success is when a person becomes what they are because that's what they always wanted to be. It could be a doctor who always saw himself healing people, the lawyer who always saw herself winning court cases, the carpenter who always saw himself building beautiful structures, the truck driver who always saw himself delivering cargo on time and the teacher who always saw herself educating and empowering students. These people are what they are because that's what they always wanted to be. Now that's success! If this is true, then why are there so many people living with unfulfilled dreams? The other group of people left home in the morning, only to come home depressed and hopeless. What happened to their dream?

> I believe that the true meaning of success is when a person becomes what they've always wanted to be.

There are many things that can hinder or devastate a person's dream. But one of the most common but least talked about is the Spirit of Debt. In our country, it has been said that 20% of the people control 80% of the wealth. That must mean that 80% of the people try to live their dreams on the 20% that's left. Is there any wonder why there is so much despair in the hearts of people today? We have all sorts of Financial Planners, talk shows and books on finances and yet poverty is reaching an all time high in our country. We even have new classifications of poor people, such as the "working poor." They have jobs but often have to choose between basic necessities such as food, gas or heat. In the case of the uninsured worker, one illness or medical bill can wipe out everything they have.

We usually think of these people, those struggling with debt, as minimum wage earners. But today that's not necessarily the situation. In the desperate search for happiness, there are people who have six figure incomes and above but are so far in debt, they are one-step away from poverty. They live in quiet desperation, trying to maintain an image that is often destroying their lives. It is better known as *keeping up with the Joneses* (as a matter of fact, they are the Joneses). When we drive through their neighborhoods, we make statements such as, "I wish I had a house like that, I wish I had a car like that, I wish my kids could play in a yard like that." When you see them in the workplace you say, "I wish I had their job." Not knowing that every day is a day of survival for them, a day of quiet desperation.

It is said that many people are only one paycheck away from poverty. With all the financial resources that we have today, why are we losing this battle? We have a disease in our society today that is devastating our very way of life. Much like alcoholism or drug abuse thirty years ago, we have accepted it as a way of life that should be kept in the closet and no one has to know. This kind of thinking caused serious damage to families then and it is ripping our families, as well as our society, apart now! I believe the driving force behind the devastating phenomenon of debt is the Spirit of Debt. What is the Spirit of Debt? Before we enter into that discussion, I need to share with you how I first encountered the Spirit of Debt in my life.

Back in 1986, my wife's father passed unexpectedly. He left her an inheritance and by 1988 we had spent all of the money except $10,000. We bought a Mercedes Benz, new furniture, paid off bills, and went on vacation (sound familiar). I told my wife that I did not want the remainder of her inheritance just to slip through our fingers. I wanted to honor her father and do something with the money that I thought would have made him proud. My wife agreed. We decided to buy a new house with more space and a bigger yard. I was brought up in the country and I remember having a big yard and a field on both sides of my home where I would play. Our son Jonathan was about three months old and I wanted a yard that he could run and play in so I wouldn't have to worry about him running into the street. It was a long process and after several months, we found a home that I really liked. At first my wife did not want to look at it because she was tired of getting her hopes up, only to be disappointed once again.

We had placed contracts on other houses only to have them fall through. Our realtor told me the only way I was going to find the house my wife wanted and the yard that I wanted would be to look outside the area and raise the price I was willing to pay.

After several months of looking with no success, as well as having no success in selling our home, we decided to take our house off the market and wait. I asked my realtor if she knew of any land that might be available. I was thinking of five acres for about $5,000 that we could purchase and build on later (after about five to ten years). She told me she didn't but that she did know of some lots in a very nice development. The builder wanted to sell the lots and move on to another exclusive project he was starting. She said he only had four lots to sell before he would move to the next project. She thought he probably would be willing to give me a good price. *Have you ever heard of the term, "I am all ears?"* Well, my face must have looked like a Bugs Bunny cartoon, just two big ears! I couldn't wait to hear more, and then she said the lots were three quarters of an acre to one-acre lots for about $70,000 per lot. I sat there looking like a deer in the headlights. I thought to myself, she has to be kidding - there is no way we can afford that! I told my realtor there must be a misunderstanding. I had said about five acres for $5,000. She said she had heard me but that this was all the land she knew of that was available in the area. She gave me the directions to the subdivision and suggested that my wife and I go take a look at the lots that were available. She did not need to give me the directions because I already knew that there was no way we could afford anything in that area. They wanted almost as much for the lot as we were hoping to pay for the house. My wife and I resigned ourselves to the fact that we would stay where we were. After all, it was a new subdivision (only five years old), we bought our house brand new and we could afford it. I just wanted to do something with the remainder of the inheritance money that would honor her father and not blow it.

Approximately two weeks later, we were on our way to see my father about 45 minutes away. As we were traveling, I asked my wife, "Where is that subdivision that our realtor had told us about? I want to see this lot that someone would buy for $70,000 for less than an acre of land." You must understand, at that time it was far beyond my financial capability, or so I thought. We turned into this street and the beautiful sign read "Winders Pond." Next to it was a beautiful pond big enough to be a lake. As we drove down the street looking for the lots, we saw large, beautiful homes and people who were smiling and waving. I thought to myself, this place is beautiful! What would it take to live in a place like this?"

Then I saw it! It was this beautiful house with a big yard and a (For Sale) sign written on a piece of wood and nailed to a tree. I drove up the long driveway, walked up to the porch and looked in the window. It was empty. I went back to the car to get my wife, totally excited about this new-found treasure—never even thinking, "Can I afford this?"

My wife just looked at me and said, "You shouldn't be peeping in people's windows."

I said, "I don't think anyone lives here. The place is empty."

The next day I called our realtor and she scheduled an appointment for me to see the house. A few days later, I met with the realtor at the house. My wife did not want to go because she felt we couldn't afford it. In addition, there was still the matter of us selling the house we had (known as a contingency, we couldn't buy another house without first selling our house). As I walked through the house, I was amazed. It had everything my wife and I wanted in a house. It had a large front yard as well as a large backyard! And not only that, it was brand new. It was as if God himself had placed it there just for us. I was so excited I couldn't wait to show the house to my wife. But first, I had to ask the question that I really wanted to avoid a little longer. How much? When the realtor told me the price, my mind began to calculate like a Pentium 4 processor because the price was almost three times more than our current mortgage.

A thought came to me, "trade in my old house for the new house." After all, they do it with cars all the time. And, since it was with the same builder that built my present house, he would know the quality of my present home. Also, it was the end of the year and they wanted to get into that new subdivision. They didn't want to pay taxes on this house if they didn't have to. Besides, they could easily find more qualified buyers for my house than for this house. It was amazing how the thoughts kept coming, providing me with a solution to having my dream.

I proposed this idea to my realtor who said, "I don't think they will do something like that. I have never heard of anyone trading in a house for a new one." I told our agent to try submitting it to the listing agent anyway and she did. While waiting for an answer from my realtor I convinced my wife to see the house. She fell in love with it. When I told her how much it would cost, she said, "How can we afford that?"

We have always had a budget every since we were first married (but we never lived by it). I told my wife that we would have $100.00 left every month after all the bills were paid. I also told her that I had talked with some successful guys at work about the house and they told me to go for it.

One guy, John, who had several businesses of his own, told me, "If you have to eat beans in the winter and salad in the summer go for it! It will be well worth it in the end."

However, I did not tell them it was an adjustable rate mortgage. That was the only way I would be able to qualify to be approved for the loan. About two days later, my realtor called me and said that our offer had been accepted! We were excited and couldn't wait to move into our new home (I later named it my *Faith Dome*). During the next two weeks, we pooled all the money we had for the down payment, including selling my wife's Mercedes. On New Years Eve of 1988, we moved into our new home (our dream come true). Little did we know that our dream was about to become a nightmare brought to us by the Spirit of Debt.

After living in our new home for only a few weeks, the expenses began to increase. We needed coverings for the windows (eighteen of them). And of course, we couldn't have just any coverings for a house like this. I wanted regular blinds until we could afford more but my wife told me that I couldn't do that in a house like this. I am a country boy who knows nothing about fashion except that it costs a lot. And a lot of money was something we did not have. Remember, we only had one hundred dollars left after living expenses were paid. But I agreed with my wife and she ordered custom-made window treatments for the house. We decided that we would put it on our credit card and, of course, pay it off in a few months by working overtime and using our tax return. Sounds like a great plan doesn't it? I also found out why they call them window treatments rather than curtains. When they are curtains, you can afford them. When they become window treatments, you need a treatment to get over the price!

Now that we had our window treatments, we realized we needed to fence in the backyard for our dog (an Alaskan malamute). Of course, we put it on our credit card. During the next several months, we realized we needed a new washer and dryer, a riding lawn mower to cut the big yard, a new king size bed because our old bed was too small for our new twenty foot by twenty foot bedroom and walk- in closet, vanity area with double sinks and a bathroom with a Japanese soak tub and glass shower.

My wife told me, "Things have to be in proportion with the room. You have no sense of fashion or design." She was right but did she have a sense of how we were going to pay all this money back?

After several months of being home with our son on maternity leave, my wife had to return to work as a Flight Attendant. Now we needed to purchase a second car for me to get to work every day. (Remember, we sold our other car to afford the down payment on the house). After about a year and many other purchases, our credit cards had reached their limit. Also, there had been an adjustment of a hundred dollars more a month to our adjustable rate mortgage. We also had to find childcare for our son. Things were really beginning to escalate and I had no means of keeping up with this runaway train.

We found ourselves in a deficit of about eight hundred dollars a month. That's right, we owed eight hundred dollars a month more after we had paid out all of the money that my wife and I had earned. In ushers the Spirit of Debt! I did not know anything about the Spirit of Debt at this time. I just thought that I was stupid, irresponsible and had made a lot of bad decisions. Why did I feel like such a failure? How could I have led my family down this path of destruction? The Spirit of Debt always wants to isolate you. We will talk more about this later.

So week after week, I would go to work *and pray I could work overtime just to stay afloat.* My wife and I would argue whenever she wanted to spend money for things like doctor's visits because my son had a cold or a low-grade fever. She was a new Mom and didn't know what to do. I would ask, "Why are you always running to the doctor's office? When I was a kid, my dad just gave us this and that."

When she mentioned something about the car not working properly, like the brakes did not feel right or the steering was pulling to the left, I didn't believe it was that serious. God forbid if she mentioned anything about getting her hair or her nails done, then the snow cone really hit the fan! I would remind her of all the money she wasted trying to make our home look beautiful (and that I had agreed with). Isn't it amazing how easy it is to pass the blame on to someone else when we are under pressure? Week after week, I lived in quiet desperation, playing the "beat the check to the bank game." I hated payday because I already knew that all my money was spent before I received my paycheck. I would try to pay one credit card with another because I knew the other credit card had just recorded my payment. I would go to the teller I knew very well at the bank and try to make a cash withdrawal off of a credit card that I knew was over the limit. I would talk to her and hope that she wouldn't check my balance because I needed the money to help me pay my mortgage. (I am not proud of having used people in this way, but desperate people will do desperate things when the Spirit of Debt is involved).

One day at work, Jim, a co-worker, came into my office to talk to one of the guys who worked there named Jake. I couldn't help but overhear their conversation because we worked in an open floor plan and Jake's desk was next to mine. I had seen Jim before in several project planning meetings or POD (plan of the day) meetings. It was easy for me to recognize him because we were often the only two people of color in the meeting. I also had seen Jim about a week before driving through our neighborhood while I was cutting my lawn. He did not recognize me, but I recognized him. The thing that got my attention the most was that Jim was driving a nice car, and there was this beautiful woman with him (his wife) and she had this happy smile on her face. I thought to myself, "He has a good life."

When I saw Jim in my office talking to my co-worker, I overheard him talking about God and how things were going in the church and what God was doing in their lives. I became very curious because I had worked around Jake for several months and I did not want anything to do with church or a Christian life after watching Jake at work. Jake talked about God all the time, he would always tell me about what he did at church over the weekend and how God was going to bless him. He had a tax preparation business on the side and he would often talk about how it was going to get him out of the shipyard.

Jake talked about loving God and treating people right on the one hand and on the other hand, he would constantly talk about upper management and how unfair the system was to minorities, especially black people. Jake would constantly be at odds with our co-workers, every time someone would point out an error that he made, it was often considered racist or an attack on his character. Racism did exist but not in this case.

Jake would often spend a lot of time preparing tax documents and making phone calls for his business during working hours. Whenever a co-worker would challenge him about spending too much company time on personal business, he would get very upset and agitated. I would ask myself, "Where is all the love for people that Jake is always preaching to me about? How can you expect other people to cover your work while you talk on the phone or prepare documents that aren't job related? How can you say you love people when you are threatening them at the same time?" I thought to myself, "If this is your God, I don't want any part of him!" I like people who say what they mean and mean what they say.

I also remembered a local preacher from years ago who was having an affair with a neighbor. I had his empty gallon Jim Beam bottles (a type of Scotch) that my neighbor had given me to put coins in. I felt the only thing different between that pastor and I was that he went to church. (I am not trying to judge anyone but these were my reasons for staying away from the church).

I remember one Monday morning, Jake was explaining to the other guys in the office how he had been at church all day Sunday, from sun up to sun down. I remember saying to myself, "Evidently he doesn't have much of a life." How wrong I was.

Now back to my first meeting with Jim. When Jim left the office that day, I followed him outside. I couldn't help but remember seeing how happy he and his wife looked as they were driving through our neighborhood. He was also one of the top nuclear construction supervisors on the job. I wanted to know more about this God he was talking about.

I called out to him, "Hey Jim can I talk to you for a minute?"

He said, "Sure, how can I help you?"

I said to Jim, "I couldn't help but overhear your conversation with Jake back in the office. Do you guys go to the same church?"

He said, "Yes we do."

I asked, "Then how come when you talk it seems like two different languages?"

He just laughed and said Jake had different ways of doing things. He never once said anything bad about Jake. As we continued to talk, Jim invited me to a Christmas play at his church. His wife had written it and was also directing the play. I agreed to come, and he gave me four tickets to the play for my wife and I and a couple of friends. Little did I know that my life would be forever changed. I know you are asking, "What does this have to do with debt?" **If you want to win the battle, everything!**

On Saturday night, my wife and I invited two friends to go see a play and to have dinner and drinks afterwards. After all, it was very nice of Jim to offer us these free tickets. I was quite sure it would be a good way to get in the Christmas spirit and, again, it was free. I thought it would be like a good high school play and remember, I wanted to get on Jim's good side. Then I could begin to learn how to be successful like him. I would be able to afford nice things and my beautiful wife could have a smile on her face rather than the pain from the burden of debt that we were carrying. When we arrived at the church, I was in for a surprise. I did not know that it was the largest church in the city. I thought to myself, "This place is huge."

When we went inside the church, we saw how it was beautifully adorned with Christmas decorations and beautiful Christmas trees. The ushers were very friendly and showed us to our seats. The place was packed with people. I didn't think that many people would give up partying on a Saturday night to come to something like this. Then a guy comes up to the stage, welcomes everyone and the play begins. This huge curtain begins to rise and all the people dressed in beautiful costumes begin to sing. The background was beautifully painted as though you were really there in Bethlehem when Christ was born.

I remember this one big guy who had an incredible voice. He reminded me of the movie Stir Crazy, with Gene Wilder and Richard Prior; back in the eighties. There was this guy in the prison cell with Gene Wilder. He was about six-foot, three-inches tall and weighed about three hundred pounds. This guy had a voice that was incredible and it resonated throughout the prison whenever he sang. The guy in the play reminded me of him. The people portraying Mary and Joseph in the play also had great voices.

I was sitting next to my friend Jim and I asked him, "Do they get paid for this?"

He laughed and said, "No, they are all volunteers from our church."

"I couldn't get over it!" I said to Jim, "They are as good as Broadway actors. Are you sure that they don't get paid for this?" He assured me that they were not professionals, just volunteers.

About that time, the Pastor came on stage, just before the grand finale and made an altar call, "If you believe that Jesus was born and died for you and you want forgiveness for your sins and eternal life, come down to the front I want to pray for you."

I just sat there like a bump on a log. Then, the Pastor said it again and still I sat there. I thought to myself, what would my friends think who came with us? They won't want to hang out with us anymore. Then, I said to myself, okay God, if the Pastor does it one more time, I am going down there.

Then the Pastor said, "Jesus said if you are ashamed of me before men, then I will be ashamed of you before the Father!" (Luke 9:26). I still sat there and I said to myself, I should have gone. I blew it!

Then the Pastor said it again and I said to myself, "I don't care what anybody thinks. I am going down to ask Jesus to come into my life forever!"

I don't know where you are at this point in your life. But I knew mine was a mess and I needed more than my *genius* to fix this mess. I realized that it was my so-called genius that got us into this mess. I had a beautiful wife, lived in an affluent neighborhood, and had a good job. It all looked good on the outside. But the truth was, my marriage and everything that I had worked so hard for was coming apart at the seams. There is an old saying: "Look good, smell good and broke." I knew that I was not at this play by chance. I realized that it was God who had set up this divine appointment. I needed Jesus in my life.

After we left the church that night, we went to a local restaurant and ordered dinner. Everyone else ordered drinks. I would normally have ordered a Johnny Walker Red (Scotch) and Coke, but I remembered a passage in the Bible that read "Don't be drunk." Well, I thought by the time I figured out that I was drunk, then it would be too late. So I quit drinking that night. Eighteen years ago! The real miracle was that I knew that scripture, since I knew very little about the Bible at that time. God had already begun to change my life.

> I had a beautiful wife, lived in an affluent neighborhood, and had a good job. It all looked good on the outside. But the truth was, my marriage and everything that I had worked so hard for was coming apart at the seams.

CHAPTER 2

Encountering the Spirit of Debt

A fter going to my friend Jim's church for several weeks, I told him that it was too big for me. The churches that I was used to attending were little country churches, with an attendance of about one hundred to two hundred people. Jim's church had about two thousand people in attendance. I really felt lost. Jim told me about a new church that a friend of his had just started pastoring. He told me that the pastor was also named Jim. He was a retired banker from a large bank in New York and they had been friends for about twenty years. I thought this was great because not only could he teach me about the Bible, he could also help me get out of the financial quicksand that I was in! Who else would know better how to get out of debt than a banker? Especially a retired Vice President and a Pastor too. This was great!

The next Sunday I went to Pastor Jim's church for the first time. My friend, Jim, told me to ask for a guy named Carl and that he would be expecting me. Jim said that he and Carl had been friends since childhood and that he would take care of me. When I asked the lady at the door for someone named Carl, she responded with a smile and said, "I will be right back."

She returned with this guy with a big smile on his face who said, "Hi, I am Carl." I told him my name and that Jim had sent me to visit their church. He said, "Sure, come on in."

I sat there with Carl and his wife, Louise, not knowing what to expect because Jim's church had been the first church that I had attended in years. This particular Sunday was Youth Sunday and they had a contest for the youth to show how well they knew the Bible scriptures. I was very impressed with the artwork and their knowledge of the Bible, since they were so young. I thought to myself, "I can learn a lot by attending this church. It is not too big and the people seemed very warm."

After the service ended, Carl took me around and introduced me to some of the people and then he took me over to meet Pastor Jim. He was a distinguished looking man with a touch of gray on the sides of his hair. He was very well- spoken and his smile was warm and welcoming. Pastor Jim made me feel as if I was already a part of his church family.

I couldn't wait to go home and tell my wife about the new church that I had found. I knew she was waiting to hear about my visit. Sure enough, when I got home she said, "Well, what happened?"

I began to tell her all about the events of the day, how nice the people had been to me, how real Carl seemed to be, how smart the children were and what a nice man Pastor Jim was. I told her, "You know, a church like this would be a good place for our (year old) son to grow up. Also, Pastor Jim is a banker. I know he can tell me how to get out of this mess that we are in."

A few weeks before, I had been watching television. I saw a show that talked about how to become debt free. I was intrigued and ordered the free book. I was all for anything that could help me get out of the mess that I was in. As soon as the book arrived in the mail, I started reading it. It was talking about something called tithing. I had never heard of this before. It had something to do with giving the preacher 10% of your money. I read the booklet, but I still couldn't make any sense out of how this was supposed to work. I told my wife about it and she gave me a look as if I had just grown two heads. I knew that if anybody knew about this tithe thing, it would be the pastor.

Rather than wait to see the pastor, I said to myself, "I know who would know about this tithe thing. My friend Jim, he knows everything there is to know about the Bible. I know that he knows all about tithing and how it works, especially the part about getting me out of debt." I called Jim on the phone and he agreed to meet me at a local restaurant. We had a very in-depth conversation about God and tithing. Jim was very patient and answered all my questions. I know that some of my questions must have seemed a little silly to him, but I had no idea about this tithe thing. After a couple of hours of discussion, Jim and I went our separate ways. I thought to myself, this thing still doesn't make any sense."

I tried to understand, but I just didn't get it. I thought to myself if we attended the church for a few more weeks and Pastor Jim got to know us a little better, I would pull him aside and ask him about this tithing thing. After all, this must be exclusive, only for certain people, or anyone would be able to understand it.

The next week, I took my family back to the church and my wife met the church's people for the first time. They were very gracious and warm. Carl's wife came over to us, took our young son and held him the entire service. She treated him as though he was one of her own children. Carl and his wife had two wonderful teenage children, a girl and a boy. I guess Carl's wife could have been missing the time when theirs were that young. Their children took to our son and he was enjoying every minute! I knew that I was in the right place. My wife liked the women there and she seemed to be enjoying the service.

Later, when we got home, I asked my wife, "What did you think about the church?"

"Well," she said, "the Pastor is a good teacher, the people seem nice and our son really gets along with the other kids. I think it's worth a try."

The next Sunday, we went back to the church. I thought this would be the Sunday I would ask the pastor about tithing. After the church service was over, one of the ladies asked, "Where did you say you lived?"

I said, "In Winders Pond."

She began to tell several people, "Do you know where they live? At the Pond! Where all those beautiful houses are? How long have you lived there? You know, we thought about moving there but it was just too expensive. Those are really some beautiful homes."

She kept talking about the neighborhood. She was right. It was a premier neighborhood at that time. But little did she know that we could not afford it.

You see, we had all the trappings of success: a luxury car, new house, and my wife had a carat and half diamond ring, not to mention the gold jewelry. Yes, we looked good, smelled good and we were broke. I knew that it would be harder now for me to talk to the pastor about finances. After all, we look like we've got it all. Isn't it amazing how we want to keep up appearances, even when we know we are going down for the count? My wife is a very private person. I knew that it would be hard for her to let anyone know about our financial situation, especially a pastor. But I didn't see it that way. I saw a banker who happened to be a pastor. To me that meant that he had to be an honest banker. How could I lose, with a deal like this?

The following week I was watching television and a pastor was on the show talking about God's financial plan. I didn't know that God had any money. Let alone a plan on how to use it. I said to myself, "This is just another preacher trying to get some money!" I changed the channel. Then a thought popped into my head, "Why don't you watch it and see what he has to say?" So I turned back and watched the program in its entirety. When the program was over, I had more questions than before about my finances. When I was saved a few months ago at church, the preacher talked to me about eternal life and when I get to heaven. But this guy was talking about benefits here now, on earth. I was really confused.

So I called Pastor Jim and asked him if I could meet with him. He said that he would meet me at the Club House (where we held our church meetings). I met with him and for about two hours, he explained to me about tithes and God's financial plan. He was a very good teacher and he knew how to simplify things so one could grasp the concept. Many of the things he told me about tithing were the same things my friend, Jim, had told me, but I still couldn't get it. After the meeting, I went home and sat in my office, looking at all the bills, wondering how long I could keep this up before I went under. How long could I work every minute of overtime that I could grab, keep switching credit cards (they were all maxed out or cancelled), and most of all, keep lying to myself and to my family, that it's going to get better ? No, it isn't!

I put my head in my hands and said, "God, I hear you have a financial plan. I also hear that you require 10% of my income (the tithe) in order for this plan to work. God, I have talked to my friend, Jim, my pastor (your representative), and I still don't understand. God, how am I going to give you 10% when we have an eight hundred dollar a month deficit? The only thing that I have close to 10% is the money that I am putting into my 401k plan at work. They are matching me dollar for dollar. Any fool would know that you don't give up something that's matching you dollar for dollar."

What happened next would change my life forever! I heard a voice say to me, **"Are you going to believe me or Wall Street?"** You must remember that I am a new Christian, of only a few months. All of this is new to me. I don't know anything about the voice of the Holy Spirit, God talking to people or any other *"Christianeese."* But I know what I heard: "Are you going to believe me or Wall Street?" Then the thought came to me, go to my Bible and turn to Psalm 50:15.

I need to take a minute to explain to you about this specific Bible that I am referring to. Several years before, we had some friends who gave us this Bible (the New King James version) as a birthday gift. Because my wife's birthday is on the sixth and my birthday is the seventh of July, this was something of a joint birthday gift. I remember asking my wife after our friends had left, "Why did they give us this? At least they could have given me a six pack of beer or a bottle of Johnny Walker Red - something I could use." Stupid comes in all shapes and sizes!

Here I am several years later, reaching for that same Bible (the only Bible I had) to look up Psalm 50:15. This is what it said, "Call upon me in the day of trouble; I will deliver you and you shall glorify Me." After reading that scripture, I said, "Wait a minute, God! Do you mean to tell me that you will get me out of this mess and all I have to do is tell people that you did it? God, I will tithe and if it means that I will have to stop my 401K to do it, then so be it."

Then I ran downstairs to share with my wife what God just told me (some things are better kept quiet until you can explain them). What she said to me, well, I cannot repeat in this book! The bottom line was, "So now you're going to give away money that we don't have to the preacher?"

I understood from her point of view. It was my genius that had gotten us into this mess in the first place and now the only savings we had was my 401K. I was going to stop that and give it to the preacher. I knew that my wife was so angry with me that she might take our son and walk out of the door without looking back. I had to make a decision to trust God! We may not know all the answers. Sometimes you have to act on what you do know. I call it the Blind Man's Club.

The Bible says "Jesus Heals a Man Born Blind,

"As he went along, he saw a man blind from birth. His disciples asked him, "Rabbi, who sinned, this man or his parents, that he was born blind?" Neither this man nor his parents sinned," said Jesus, "but this happened so that the work of God might be displayed in his life. As long as it is day, we must do the work of him who sent me. Night is coming, when no one can work. While I am in the world, I am the light of the world. Having said this, he spit on the ground, made some mud with the saliva, and put it on the man's eyes. Go," he told him, "wash in the Pool of Siloam" (this word means Sent). So the man went and washed, and came home seeing. His neighbors and those who had formerly seen him begging asked, "Isn't this the same man who used to sit and beg? "Some claimed that he was. Others said, "No, he only looks like him." But he himself insisted, "I am the man." "How then were your eyes opened?" they demanded. He replied, "The man they call Jesus made some mud and put it on my eyes. He told me to go to Siloam and wash. So I went and washed, and then I could see. "Where is this man?" they asked him. "I don't know," he said."

The Pharisees Investigate the Healing

"They brought to the Pharisees the man who had been blind. Now the day on which Jesus had made the mud and opened the man's eyes was a Sabbath. Therefore the Pharisees also asked him how he had received his sight. "He put mud on my eyes," the man replied, "and I washed, and now I see." Some of the Pharisees said, "This man is not from God, for he does not keep the Sabbath." But others asked, "How can a sinner do such miraculous signs?" So they were divided. Finally they turned again to the blind man, "What have you to say about him? It was your eyes he opened." The man replied, "He is a prophet." The Jews still did not believe that he had been blind and had received his sight until they sent for the man's parents. "Is this your son?" they asked. "Is this the one you say was born blind? How is it that now he can see?" "We know he is our son," the parents answered, "and we know he was born blind. But how he can see now, or who opened his eyes, we don't know. Ask him. He is of age; he will speak for himself." His parents said this because they were afraid of the Jews, for already the Jews had decided that anyone who acknowledged that Jesus was the Christ would be put out of the synagogue. That was why his parents said, "He is of age; ask him." A second time they summoned the man who had been blind. "Give glory to God, "they said." We know this man is a sinner." He replied, "Whether he is a sinner or not, I don't know. One thing I do know. I was blind but now I see!" (John 9:1-25).

When Jesus healed the blind man in the Bible, the Bible says that the Pharisees and Sadducees questioned him about how he got his sight back. They also questioned him about who Jesus was. After several questions, the blind man said (and I am paraphrasing), I don't know who he is. All I know is this, "that once I was blind and now I can see!" You do the math I am out of here."

Several weeks had passed and I was still in debt. My wife had not left me, although I don't think she had abandoned the idea just yet. I was tithing. Somehow, every pay period, I had enough money to bring my tithe to God and place it in the offering plate at church. About a week later, I noticed that our car badly needed a new tire. I thought that something was wrong with the tire because it had worn out too soon. I drove the car to the Sears service center where I had purchased the tire. I had been having my cars serviced at Sears for several years and I knew the shop manager personally. I was hoping that the tire would be still under warranty because I did not have the money to replace it.

When I walked into Sears, the shop manager met me with a smile, as he always did, he said, "Well, Frank, it's great to see you again. How is the family? And how can I help you today?"

I told him what the problem was and that I believed the tire was still under warranty. He said, "Let's take a look at it." After he examined the car, he said, "Well, you are right. The tire is bad but that's because your shocks are bad and that's because your springs are bad. So when the shocks failed, it caused the weight of the car to fall completely on the springs, causing the springs to fail and leaving all of the weight on your tires and that's what caused the tires to wear out so quickly."

I stood there, cool and calm on the outside, like no big deal. I was thinking, just do what needs to be done to fix the problem and I will pay the bill and be on my way. But on the inside, I was thinking, "This has to be a bad dream! I need this car for my wife to get to work. She can't drive the other car to the airport - it is not dependable enough to drive that distance. Besides, I just started tithing! God, I thought things like this weren't supposed to happen. God, I am trusting in you! How am I going to get the money to pay for these repairs? What am I going to do now?"

I asked how much would it cost? He wrote up an estimate for me and said, "Here you are," and handed it over. It was for five hundred and two dollars (in 1990 that was a lot of money). I wanted to faint. My suave debonair look had fallen by the wayside and all that was left must have been sheer panic on my face.

I said, "This much? That's a lot!"

He took one look at me and said, "Wait a minute, let me take a look at something here."

I stood there with my mind turning one hundred miles an hour, trying to figure out a way to pay for these repairs. Then he looked up at me (from his computer) and he said, **"Because the covered part caused the non-covered part to fail, then the non-covered part is now covered."** Now would you like to say that three times, very quickly? I did not care if it did sound like a riddle, I was a happy man. They replaced my shocks, the springs and the tires. When I walked up to the cashier, my bill read, "Paid in Full under Warranty." I wanted to jump up on the counter and scream, "It works! Tithing works!" God had given me favor. You can say what you want about tithing, but I belong to the Blind Man's Club!

This is not a book on tithing but without the tithe, you will never defeat the Spirit of Debt. I am sharing with you how I came to find out about this phenomenal destructive force (the Spirit of Debt) in my life and how I discovered the power to destroy it's affect on my life. A discovery that I believe, in sharing, can help free other people that are caught in the same destructive force.

How about you? Are you tired of the struggling, the family arguments, and living in quiet desperation? Are you sick and tired of being sick and tired? Just ask Jesus to forgive you of your sins and come into your life and he will!

About a week later, someone asked me if I had read a book called "War On Debt," by John Avanzini? I hadn't and I asked about him. He said that Avanzini taught about prosperity and God's financial plan and "The War on Debt" was his new book. I thought about how I would love learning about God's financial plan. A week later, I obtained the book and began to read it. Now, I never considered myself much of a reader. However, what I found out about myself was that it wasn't that I didn't like to read, but it really depended on what I was reading. If you handed me the book War and Peace to read, shortly you would find me asleep. But, if you gave me a book on finances, then I wouldn't put it down. As I began to read The War on Debt, it started explaining the different reasons people were in debt. As I continued to read, the title to the next chapter read the "Spirit of Debt." I had never heard of this before. I thought to myself, "What is that? Some kind of ghost or what?" The only spirit I knew was the Spirit of God. I had heard of evil spirits but thank God I had never encountered one. As I kept on reading about this Spirit of Debt, I recognized more and more how much my life had been totally affected by it but I had no idea that it even existed.

This is why I wanted to tell you my story. How many people struggle with debt from day to day? Blaming themselves or their spouses for poor money management decisions, never realizing how the Spirit of Debt is impacting their lives. So let's take a closer look at this problem and see if we can recognize how this is affecting your life. Let's expose this destructive force that has wreaked havoc in so many people's lives.

CHAPTER 3

Identifying the Spirit of Debt

How do we identify the Spirit of Debt? As children, most of us had dreams. We dreamed of becoming: lawyers, doctors, teachers, athletes, astronauts, writers, etc. We have all heard, especially in America, the age-old adage of "get an education and get a good job." We all dreamed of the day when we would grow up and become independent. We would have our own money, live in our own place and make our own decisions. We thought, "I just can't wait until I am old enough!"

Today we are living in a society that is filled with people who are frustrated, discouraged and even hopeless. They are living from paycheck to paycheck, and week to week. Their dreams and ambitions have all but disappeared under the ever-mounting influence of the Spirit of Debt. We live in a world where the joy of life seems like only an illusion, like trying to catch a handful of smoke. What happened?

Remember the day when you had your first job and in about two weeks, you would receive your very first paycheck? Do you remember the joy you had, just thinking about all the things you were going to do with that first paycheck? Things like buying new shoes, new clothes, and new rims for your car, a gift for your parents or maybe that special friend. You were so excited about the possibilities!

Now, many years later, and a lot more money earned than that first paycheck, when we think of payday, all that joy no longer exists. We may even feel depressed that payday is here because the Spirit of Debt has robbed us of our joy.

Let's talk about some other ways the Spirit of Debt affects our lives. How about impulse spending? You know, things like unplanned vacations, such as when your friends call up and tell you about a great deal they got to go to the Bahamas for three nights and four days. It was only ninety-nine dollars for airfare! Not to mention nine hundred dollars for hotel, food and entertainment. Not to mention transportation.

We take weekend getaways, and say to ourselves, "I (key word "I") deserve it! After all, I worked hard all week. Besides, the card is almost at the maximum anyway. Another couple of hundred dollars won't make a difference."

Ladies, or that shopping spree, when the girls stop by on their way to the mall for that 50% off red tag sale. (I wonder why they are always red tags? Could it be because it represents danger?) You know that you shouldn't go but that little voice inside your head says, "What will they think if you tell them that you can't afford it? That you don't have the money? If you don't go, you're going to miss out on all the sales! You need a break from being with the kids and working all week. And think how much money you will save." How about the great Buy One, Get One Free sale? That has to be the *grand-daddy* of them all! Now you can have two of what you didn't need in the first place.

Isn't it amazing how we talk ourselves into these things? But is it really us doing the talking? Did you ever stop to think where these thoughts come from? Have you ever found yourself talking aloud-saying things like, "That's right, I do deserve it?" Or "I am going to get it anyway." Some people call this self-talk. My question is not only, "Who are you talking to?" But also, "Who's asking the questions?" Isn't it strange that usually when it comes to spending, especially money that we don't have there is always a conversation that goes on in our heads?

I remember cutting my yard on a hot summer's day. It was our first summer in our new home. We had a very large yard and it took me almost four hours to cut the grass and trim the edges. I always liked a well manicured lawn so I would give a lot of attention to detail. One day my wife asked me "Why does it take you so long to cut the grass"? My first thought was "If you would come out and help me then it wouldn't take so long." My wife had tried to help me before, but I re-worked everything she had done, that's when she said, "That's it I am going back into the house."

My wife talked about buying a riding lawn mower because the yard was so large. I told her that we did not need it because this push lawn mower was just fine, besides we don't have the money to buy a riding mower. I could probably have made it easier by cutting the front yard one day and the backyard the next day. However, I wanted to get it all done at one time.

About a week later I saw my neighbor was cutting his lawn on his brand new riding lawn mower, it was a Toro. He was just riding along with a big smile on his face. All I could see in my mind was a picture of that Toro commercial, where the guy in the commercial was riding along with a big smile on his face, while his neighbor was pushing his lawn mower with sweat pouring off him about to collapse. All of sudden I saw myself pushing my lawn mower, sweat was pouring off and I felt like I was about to drop. Then, a voice (a thought) in my head said to me "Why are you killing yourself pushing this mower?" You deserve a new riding mower too!" Then, I looked over at my neighbor and he was still riding and smiling. Then, I said to myself, "That would be nice, but I can't afford it." Then, I look across the street again and my neighbor was gone. He had finished cutting his lawn and I was still working on the front lawn.

That's when I said, "That's it! I am getting myself a rider; I am not going to push this mower anymore." I did not take into consideration that my neighbor's lawn was half the size of my lawn. When the Spirit of Debt speaks to you all rational thinking gets blocked out by the "I wants." So I thought I can't afford a new mower, but I can maybe find a good used riding lawn mower. That makes sense right? Wrong! I couldn't afford any mower because we had just bought a new house and tripled our mortgage.

Nevertheless, I looked around for about two weeks and found a really good used riding lawn mower (so I thought). I ended up spending more money in repairs on that so- called good used riding lawn mower, than I would have if I had bought two new riding lawn mowers. If I had listened to the voice of reason, then I would have cut the front yard one day and the backyard the next day, until I was financially able to buy a new riding lawn mower with a warranty. Be careful to identify the voice (the conversation) you are listening to in your head!

We find ourselves living from paycheck to paycheck. Is it really living or would it be more appropriate to call it existing from paycheck to paycheck? We also call it the Game of Life, playing games just to survive; games such as the old "Beat the Check to the Bank" game. Some of us remember that more than others, depending on how old we are. If you are a baby boomer, then you remember it well and may still be playing it. If you are thirty-five or younger, then you are probably using creative methods on the internet. Today the new fad is the quick check cashing companies. They will give you an advance on your paycheck that you haven't received yet. Payday loans. Think about it, you are already in a deficit so you borrow more money to pay off the deficit.

I also love the commercials from the loan companies— especially the equity loan companies that say, "Become debt free when you take a new low interest equity loan from me and pay off all those unwanted high interest credit card bills." That's like loving the beach and hating the sand.

How many times do you sit down to pay your debts and find yourself playing the shell game? You remember that game - where you take a pea and place it under one of three shells and the object is to find the correct shell with the pea under it. That's how we treat our bills. We create several piles of bills labeled Pay Now, Pay Later, and Pay When I Can. Then, we try to find the money for the Pay Now pile or we move the piles around to the What You Can Pay pile. Sometimes, we get reduced to quoting Shakespeare (even if we haven't read Hamlet): To pay or not to pay? That is the question. Many times, there is just too much month at the end of the money.

Today in America, this is fast becoming the rule rather than the exception! We have become a nation of consumers. People who go to church and people who don't go to church are being devastated by the heavy burden of debt. The believer and the non-believer alike are struggling to find their equilibrium in this sea of debt and the high winds of an ever-changing economy. These factors are clear signs of the impact that the Spirit of Debt has on our lives. The church has failed to recognize the warning given in Ephesians 6:10-12, "Finally, be strong in the Lord and in his mighty power. Put on the full armor of God so that you can take your stand against the devil's schemes. For our struggle is not against flesh and blood, but against the rulers, against the authorities, against the powers of this dark world and against the spiritual forces of evil in heavenly realms." (NIV)

The Bible tells me that I am not struggling against flesh and blood but against spiritual forces of evil in heavenly realms. This tells me that when I am dealing with the Spirit of Debt in my life, doing natural things won't change what is accruing in the supernatural. What does that mean? Let me explain.

Earlier, I gave you an opportunity to ask Jesus Christ to come into your life. (See page 26) If you did not take advantage of that opportunity, I strongly suggest that you do it now! If you are a believer, then you already have the Spirit of God living inside of you. However, you might not be living a life pleasing to God. Again, I strongly suggest that you do it now! Repent (a decision to turn 180 degrees and go the other way) ask God for his forgiveness. Stop doing the wrong things (and start doing what is pleasing to God), for he is just and faithful to forgive us our sins.

Why am I telling you this? Because it is truly a matter of life and death! You probably already know the answer because you have tried working two jobs, working all the overtime you can get and borrowing money. Remember, I said you are not struggling with natural things but against spiritual things – supernatural things. The only thing that can defeat the supernatural is the supernatural. I don't care if you have won the triathlon and you are the strongest man in the world, you cannot defeat a baby demon. The only thing that can defeat an evil spirit is the Spirit of God. In Acts 19: 13-16 it reads, "Some Jews who went around driving out evil spirits tried to invoke the name of the Lord Jesus over those who were demon-possessed. They would say, 'In the name of Jesus, whom Paul preaches, I command you to come out.' The seven sons of Sceva, a Jewish chief priest, were doing this. One day the evil spirit answered them, 'Jesus I know, and I know about Paul, but who are you?' Then the man who had the evil spirit jumped on them and overpowered them all. He gave them such a beating that they ran out of the house naked and bleeding." This is an excellent example of why we need the power of God to obtain victory in our lives.

Proverbs 3: 13-17 reads, "Blessed is the man who finds wisdom, the man who gains understanding, for she is more profitable than silver and yields better returns than gold. She is more precious than rubies; nothing you desire can compare with her. Long life is in her right hand; in her left hand are riches and honor. Her ways are pleasant ways, and all her paths are peace." The Bible tells us that we need understanding. One of our country's greatest generals, once said, "If we are to defeat our enemy, then we first must understand our enemy." Based on that wisdom, let's take a look at how debt is introduced into our lives.

(1) How we live:

The introduction of debt to most families is very subtle. Debt surrounded us when we were children. It was almost like the very air we breathed. We were constantly in contact with it, many times depending on it for our very survival. As children, we did not know how it worked or where it came from. As children we did not care.

As Adults, we raise our children in a home that is mortgaged. We drive them in a car that is financed. They sleep in beds that are financed. They wear clothes and shoes that are financed. We wash and dry their clothes with a washer and a dryer that are financed. The television programs are watched on a television set (Excuse me, an entertainment center) that is financed. Now we have passed our legacy of "debt mentality" on to our children.

(2) What we hear:

What do our children hear? "Don't forget to pay that bill. All right, we were approved for the loan! God has blessed us with this loan (did he?). And last but not least, Visa just gave us five thousand dollars! Isn't that Great!" Wrong! Visa did not give you anything and if you don't believe me, try not paying the money back to Visa. When our children hear us say and react this way about debt and borrowing, they begin to think that debt is something good to obtain.

Their entire perception of money becomes distorted because of the message we send as parents. You may say, "I don't believe that what I say can have that kind of effect on my child" or "I don't talk about those matters in front of my children." Well, you may think they aren't aware, but they are taking it all in – even when we least expect it.

I remember one day when my son was about fifteen years old. We were discussing something (I can't remember the topic) and he said to me, "Dad, I don't know why you and mom close the door when you argue. I can still hear what you are saying."

Our children hear a lot more than we think they do. How about some of the things that you heard your parents say as a child and would not dare tell them what you heard?

Think about this, some psychologists say that two hours of sex and violence on television does not have an effect on our children. If that is a true statement, then why is the advertising industry a multi-billion dollar industry? Why does Madison Avenue spend millions of dollars for sixty seconds of commercial time during the Super Bowl or The World Series? Remember, two hours has no effect on our children but the advertisers are spending millions of dollars for a few seconds. Doesn't make much sense, does it?

You might say that you are the type of person that follows your own mind and you don't let other people's opinions affect you. Let's say that you were in my class and as your instructor, you heard me say a lot of negative things about a young man who was about six foot, nine inches tall, wore dreadlocks and had a scar on his cheek. After the class, you stopped by your local convenience store on the way home. In that store, you saw a young man who was about six foot, nine inches tall, wore dreadlocks and had a scar on his cheek. He fits my description to a tee, but this young man was doing one of the nicest things you had ever seen anyone do to help an old lady. Now you have to fight against all the negative things you heard me say earlier in the classroom. What you heard and what you are seeing is creating a conflict in your mind. That's because you had faith in what you heard me say and now you must try to get rid of the old information in order to let in the new. Now I hope you can see how powerful our spoken words are. This is especially true in the mind of a child, whose brain is like a sponge absorbing all the knowledge around them. It's usually before their right and wrong filters (the conscience) have been fully developed that these impurities imbed themselves. The Bible says, *"The tongue has the power of life and death and those who love it will eat its fruit."* (Prov. 18:21). *The Bible also says,* *"Faith comes by hearing and hearing of the word of God."* (Rom. 10:17).

(3) The Maturity Ritual:

In the Jewish culture, when a boy comes of age they have a ceremony that is called a bar mitzvah. This is a ceremony that recognizes and initiates a thirteen-year-old child as an adult responsible for his moral and religious duties. This is a high honor in the Jewish community. In our American culture, we also have a maturity ritual. We help our children to get their first credit card in order to help them establish their own line of credit. After all, they are of age now and if they are going to get anywhere in life, they will need the ability to borrow money. We lovingly take our children and help them buy a car for about $10,000 to $20,000 on a minimum wage salary. Not to mention licenses, insurance, taxes and gas. They have just completed high school and we sentence them to hundreds of hours as a servant to the lender. That's approximately how much of their young life they must give in order to pay off their new debt. We ignore the warning that has been given in God's word:

"Train a child in the way he should go and when he is old he will not turn from it. The rich rule over the poor and the borrower is servant to the lender." (Proverbs 22:6-7).

In other words, raise a child with a borrowing mentality, and as an adult, he or she will become a slave to the lender. Think about the checkout line at the grocery store. The cashier is on one side and all the gum and candy bars are on the other side. I call it The Gauntlet. This is where the battle of wills is often tested between mother and child. How many times have you gotten into that checkout line and in front of you was a mom with a cute little toddler in the shopping cart. You remember how pretty those big eyes were and those little legs hanging out of the cart. You said to yourself, "What a little angel."

Raise a child with a borrowing mentality, and as an adult, he or she will become a slave to the lender.

Then mom pushed the cart closer to the cashier, between the conveyor belt and the gum and candy. Almost in an instant, that little angel didn't seem like an angel anymore. The child began to reach for the gum and candy and mom is saying, "No, you can't have that." Mom has now entered The Gauntlet where the only way out is to check out. For the next few minutes, mom and child have a battle of the wills as the child screams and cries "I want it!" Most of the people in line murmur under their breath or move impatiently from side to side, letting mom know that they want the kid to shut-up! Finally, out of frustration and embarrassment, mom gives in and says, "OK, you can have one."

That child has just received the first lesson in instant gratification. When that child becomes an adult, he or she would not have learned boundaries or obtained any knowledge about delayed gratification. Those candy bars eventually become cars, boats, jewelry, vacations and houses. The borrower becomes a servant to the lender. I like to say it this way, "The borrower becomes a slave to the lender." You could think, "I am not a slave to anybody and you are exaggerating" I am glad that you think that way. Let me ask you a few simple questions: Do you live in the house you always wanted to live in? Do you drive the car you always wanted to drive? Do your children go to the school of your choice? Will your children attend the college of their choice? How often do you eat at your favorite restaurant? And when was the last time you were at your favorite vacation spot? I will go so far as to ask, when was the last time you had a vacation? If you have to think about any of the questions above, it is possible that debt has a bearing on your lifestyle. Any time your debt controls how you live, well, you do the math! "The rich rule over the poor and the borrower is a servant to the lender." (Proverbs 22:7).

When children become adults, they are trapped in a revolving door. Merely existing, they are living from paycheck to paycheck controlled by the Spirit of Debt. They live a life based on lies and self-deception. So often, we try to provide an image that we cannot afford. We go out to lunches and dinners that we can't afford, attend social events, such as football games, weekend golf, theaters and ballets that we can't afford. We don't really have enough cash to buy gas to get to work but God forbid if anyone found out that we couldn't afford to drive. The little voice in our head says, "Go ahead; it's okay to put it on your credit card. Everyone knows that going to the ballet with your boss is a good career move. You are showing them that you're a team

So often, we try to provide an image that we cannot afford.

player. After all, everyone knows that most business deals are made over dinner or on the golf course. That can be considered a career investment. Remorsefully, we later tell ourselves, I know that I shouldn't have done this but... I have a saying—*butts are only good to sit on.*

Have you ever heard the saying that "The rich get richer and the poor get poorer?" Why do you think that is? Let's take for example that I am a plumber by trade. Do you believe that I could teach someone else how to be a plumber? Of course, I could because I can teach by example. What if a person came to me and requested that I teach them how to be a butcher? Do you think I can train them how to be a good butcher? Of course, I can't because I have very little, if any, knowledge of how to be a butcher. The principle here is that you cannot teach what you don't know! If you have been trained with a debt mentality, what do you think will happen? *"Train a child in the way he should go and when he is old he will not turn from it."* (Proverbs 22:6).

This is why we must learn how the Spirit of Debt operates. Not only so we can be set free from its influence but also, we can protect our children from its destructive influence. How many actors' children have become actors? An athlete whose child became an athlete? A singer whose child became a singer? A doctor whose child became a doctor? Do you get my point?

I believe that this is a biblical principle. The word of God says,

Then God said, "Let the land produce vegetation, seed-bearing plants and trees on the land that bear fruit with seed in it, according to their various kinds." And it was so. The land produced vegetation: plants bearing seed according to their kinds and trees bearing fruit with seed in it according to their kinds. And God saw that it was good. (Genesis 1:11-12).

And God said, "Let the land produce living creatures according to their kinds: livestock, creatures that move along the ground, and wild animals, each according to its kind." And it was so. God made the wild animals according to their kinds, the livestock according to their kinds, and all the creatures that move along the ground according to their kinds. And God saw that it was good." (Genesis 1:24-25).

This same principle operates just like the law of gravity, it never fails.

Now that we have a better understanding of how the Spirit of Debt is introduced to our families, I want to show you some ways that you can change your life for the better. Did you know that the same God that wants you to have salvation and eternal life through his son Jesus Christ has provided for your divine healing? He also wants you to have financial freedom: *"Beloved, I pray that you may prosper in all things and be in health, just as your soul prospers."* (3 John 1:2, NKJ) Always remember that Miracles come from the Grace of God, not by the skill of man!

CHAPTER 4

The Spirit of Debt - An Equal Opportunity Destroyer

The Spirit of Debt is an equal opportunity destroyer. We are swimming in a sea of debt and the sharks (the creditors) are circling. In America, we are drowning in a sea of debt. In 1998, bankruptcy filings broke an all time record. Within a few short years, in 2002, bankruptcy filings broke another record. The Federal Reserve Board reports that in 2006, consumer debt was at a record $2.17 trillion, and that consumers also cashed out a whopping $431 billion in home equity loans that year. Newsweek reported, **"We now have the highest level of debt to income on record since the 1950s (when the Federal Reserve Board started keeping track)."** The high rise in the cost of a college education and credit card debt has the twenty-something generation staggering like a drunk man at sea. Young people struggle to deal with The Kiss of Debt. In a report written by USA Today and The National Endowment for Financial Education (NEFE),

"High debt loads are causing anxiety, too. A poll of twenty-something's, found that 60% feel they're facing tougher financial pressure than young people did in the previous generation. And 30% say that they frequently worry about their debt." "I have nightmares," says one student who has accrued $165,000 in student loans to become a chiropractor.

We have runaway medical expenses and a Medicare program that is badly in need of an overhaul. The first of about 78 million baby boomers (born between 1946 and 1964) are due to retire in approximately 2008 or 2011. They will be depending on a Social Security program that has been out-dated, to say the least, for more than a decade. In 2004 alone, federal spending on Medicare and Social Security increased from approximately

$45 billion to about $789 billion, this was the largest premium increase in the program's thirty-nine year history. Laurence Kotlikoff, a Boston University economist and co-author of The Coming Generational Storm an article in USA Today, reported this.

Debt the spiritual predator has been devouring our financial health and well–being for many decades. The Spirit of Debt affects countries as well as households. Take a look at the past two decades. Do you remember the big Savings and Loans (S&L) scandal that caused millions of people to lose their savings because of bad S&L practices? There was an array of white-collar crimes that stole billions of dollars from the American people. Some of the people implicated in this horrendous betrayal of American's trust went as far as the White House. It was estimated that it could cost approximately $306 billion dollars to correct the problem. That was just the estimate at the time, also stating, "That the cost could be much higher." The bill to clean up this travesty was to be the responsibility of the taxpayer.

Then there was Desert Storm. How much did it cost us to fight that war? Most people only know what they saw on their local news or read in their newspaper. At the time, I lived in Yorktown, Virginia close to the Chesapeake Bay. I worked in the local shipyard there, and have worked on just about every Nimitz class Aircraft Carrier that has been built. When the local news would show an Aircraft Carrier departing for the Persian Gulf, to encounter one of Saddam Hussein's threats or to support Desert Storm, most people would watch with great pride in our military might. I, however, would ask myself how much was this costing us (the taxpayer)? Many times when our ships arrived in the Persian Gulf, Saddam Hussein would then allow the nuclear weapons inspector's access and our ships would return home.

Why is this so important? Good question. Most people don't know that whenever you see an aircraft carrier leaving for deployment, it is never alone. There are several other ships that must accompany the aircraft carrier, including a submarine. This is what is known as a battle group. It takes several thousand men and women to operate an aircraft carrier not to mention the rest of the battle group. Can you imagine how much it costs to feed several thousand people a day? How much it costs to fuel not only the aircraft carrier but also an entire battle group? Not to mention the planes that enforced the No Fly Zones that we heard so much about? I believe that the cost was so significant that Saddam Hussein used it as an economic weapon against us. That is why several times he would defy the United Nation's orders and wait for the United States to send in a battle group.

There was also Haiti and Bosnia. During the conflict with the Serbs, our military reported that our ships were to stop using cruise missiles to destroy targets because they cost too much. Once again, the cost is passed on to the taxpayer.

The World is Drunk on Debt!

The world is drunk on debt, supplied by Satan the bartender. In the 1970s, Mexico was indebted to the United States for approximately five million dollars. By the 1990s, about twenty years later, the debt had grown to approximately one hundred million dollars. Why is this important? It is important because it was a vital tool used to win Mexico's support for the North American Foreign Trade Agreement (NAFTA). The United States used the elimination of their debt as leverage for Mexico's support. For example, if I were to come to you for help and you owed me five thousand dollars, would it not influence your decision to help me? What if I offered to forgive the debt in exchange for your help, now would I have your attention?

The approval of NAFTA has changed the face of the American economy and the way of American life forever. Not to mention the way that it has affected lives in Mexico. Along with the monetary success, it has also brought environmental issues, having a major effect on the way of life of the Mexican people. In the 1980s, America was experiencing tremendous growth and Wall Street was reaching an all time high. Then, in the late eighties, Wall Street had a correction and the Dow fell to a record low. This caused America to once again change the way we conduct business. The ethics and moral standards that made our country great were greatly compromised.

During this time, there was also a boom in the Japanese and Asian economies. These countries were experiencing tremendous growth as well. Then, in the nineties, their economies also experienced a correction and financial difficulty. The headlines read, "Asian Economy on the Verge of Collapsing."

Then there was the Y2K scare. All the computer experts were jostling over whether or not computers would shut down at the turn of the century, the year 2000. This great debate was going on for most of the nineties and America was losing more jobs and spending more money than ever before in her history.

We Spent in the Eighties and Nineties and Ignored God.

We spent in the eighties and nineties and now we are paying in the new millennium. There is an old saying that says, "If you dance to the music, you have to pay the piper." As Christians, we have also, ignored God's warning concerning irresponsible borrowing (The rich rule over the poor and the borrower is servant to the lender," Proverbs 22:7). The lender is at the world's door. Americans have made more money than ever before and are saving less money than ever before. In a recent news report on NBC Nightly News (Feb-2-2007), it was reported, "American's savings was at its lowest point in its seventy-four year history." In other words since records have been kept that tracked how much we were saving as a nation, this was the lowest point ever recorded.

You are probably asking, "Why is this so important?" I am glad you asked. You are really good! The amount we have in our savings accounts as a nation is directly tied to the banks abilities to make new loans. This definitely has an effect on new businesses, new jobs and the growth of our economy.

The former Soviet Union was one of the world's greatest powers. And it was one of the greatest threats to our way of life. As a nation, we spent trillions of dollars on defense to protect ourselves against this superpower through years of strategic planning and the building of a military arsenal. The Soviet Union collapsed mainly because of their bad economy - the Spirit of Debt. The country literally spent its way into bankruptcy.

The Spirit of Debt is an equal opportunity destroyer. Individuals as well as countries are drowning in a sea of debt. In Europe, a new currency was introduced to the world market called the Euro. This was initially implemented to be the beginning of a new world order. One currency for all of Europe was to be the beginning of a one-world order. Remember the prophecy, about the mark of the beast, found in Revelation: "He causes all, both small and great, rich and poor, free and slave, to receive a mark on their right hand or on their foreheads, and that no one may buy or sell except one who has the mark or the name of the beast, or the number of his name." (Revelations 13:16-17). This passage of scripture deals directly with the world's economy.

The internet has made it easier for the world to communicate. It has revolutionized how the world does business. We call it the information highway. Today we can do business around the world in seconds. It is a major part of the business world and every major corporation has become a part of this marketing and communication phenomenon. Have you ever heard the term "New World Alliance?" Many businesses are beginning to adopt this term.

The Trap Closes – Part 1

Christians are blindly following the world into the pit and the trap door closes behind them. The Bible says, "But their minds were blinded. For until this day the same veil remains unlifted in the reading of the Old Testament, because the veil is taken away in Christ. "But even to this day, when Moses is read, a veil lies on their heart. Nevertheless when one turns to the Lord, the veil is taken away. Now the Lord is the Spirit; and where the Spirit of the Lord is, there is liberty." (2 Corinthians 3:14–17, NKJ)

Many Christians have turned away from the principal of being good stewards of what God has blessed them with. They have chosen the path of instant gratification over discipline and common sense. Many times, as Christians, we want to fit in on our job, in our neighborhood, and at our Church. The Spirit of Debt leads us down the path of destruction with thoughts like, "I want my children to have what the neighbors' children have. After all, they deserve a vacation, a new car, private school education, a new house, I am blessed." **We have become more concerned with looking blessed than actually being blessed!** Being blinded by our own wants and desires, the Bible says, "Therefore they could not believe, because Isaiah said again "He has blinded their eyes and hardened their hearts, Lest they should see with their eyes, Lest they should understand with their hearts and turn, So that I should heal them." These things Isaiah said when he saw His glory and spoke of Him. Nevertheless even among the rulers many believed in Him, but because of the Pharisees they did not confess Him, lest they should be put out of the synagogue; for they loved the praise of men more than the praise of God." (John 12:39-43)

So often because of the desire for approval by others is so important to us (families, friends, co-workers), we compromise what we know to be the right thing to do. Although the Holy Spirit speaks to our hearts and warns us not to make that purchase, we turn him off like a light switch. We tell ourselves – we rationalize - about all of the good this will do in our lives, for our families and others. Sometimes we even get so bold as to tell God how it will help him ("You know God, if I had a bigger house, then I could have the Bible study at my house, too, and God, if I had that new minivan, then I could pick up that little old lady down the street and take her to church"). The devil is a liar! We are going under in good times!

We are drunk on spending and consumer debt is running rampant in our country. So many people are treating debt like alcohol at a social event with an open bar. We are living in a buy now/pay later society. The check is in the mail mentality. In other words, I pay when I can, if I can. We have no regard for what the Bible says, "Do not withhold good from those to whom it is due, when it is in the power of your hand to do so. Do not say to your neighbor, "Go, and come back, and tomorrow I will give it, when you have it with you" (Prov. 3:27-28). The world we live in is like a financial mine field.

All around us are signs and pictures –advertisements–that shout "No money down! Buy now, pay later! Pay nothing until next year!" Not to mention, this is already December 31st. They've even created plans that will let you buy and pay nothing for up to two years. No interest, no payments hoping that we have no common sense. Most of us can't remember what we did two weeks ago; do you really think that you are going to remember you need to make your first payment March 27th?

What was that year again? My point exactly! That's when you find out that the spinning top you were playing with is really a land mine. Because when you miss that first payment date, all the interest for the last two years will be added up, added on and due!

The number of bankruptcies in the United States has set a new record. According to News Week magazine, Aug. 9, 2006, consumer debt is at a record 2.7 trillion. We have had financial growth for the past decade. The stock market has been reaching all time highs; we have low unemployment, the lowest interest rates in thirty years and multi-billion dollar mergers. Why, then, are we in so much trouble? Why are we in debt? Remember what the Bible says, "But their minds were blinded. For until this day the same veil remains unlifted in the reading of the Old Testament, because the veil is taken away in Christ." (2 Cor. 3:14 NKJ)

The Trap Closes – Part 2

Seducing spirits cause us to follow a path of destruction without reason. The Bible says, "For we do not wrestle against flesh and blood, but against principalities, against powers, against the rulers of the darkness of this age, against spiritual hosts of wickedness in the heavenly places" (Ephesians 6:12). We are left asking ourselves, "How did I get in such a mess? What was I thinking about? I knew better than to agree to terms like that."

We often feel helpless and alone. Tearing ourselves apart with demeaning accusations (stupid, dummy, childish, brain dead, gullible) all the time forgetting that we have help. The same voice that helped you rationalize why this would be such a great idea, is the same voice, the voice of the Spirit of Debt, that is now saying, "Look what you did."

In our depressed state of mind, it is very hard to fight through our guilt. You see the truth is "for we do not wrestle against flesh and blood, but against principalities, against powers, against the rulers of the darkness of this age, against spiritual hosts of wickedness in the heavenly places." The unawareness of this reality has been the destruction of many people, Christian and non-Christian alike.

You may be saying to yourself, "I am not a Christian. I don't know if I believe all of this." I say to you, Sir, or to you, Ms., since you have read this far then, I know that you have found enough truth that kept you reading to this point. Let's take a look at the facts. I said earlier that the Spirit of Debt is an equal opportunity destroyer. That simply means it will destroy anyone regardless of race, religion, age or gender, who does not heed God's word, and does not practice good money management skills, such as financial planning. It is based on a spiritual principle.

Let's take gravity as an example. Let's say that you have never heard of the law of gravity. No one told you about it; you never read about it, you have totally no knowledge of the law of gravity. One day you went up to the roof of a ten story building and decided to jump off without an external source of flight or a parachute. You are about to have your first (and maybe your last) introduction to the law of gravity. Because you did not know about the law of gravity, it will not say to you, "I am sorry Mr. Jones. You did not know about the law so I am going to put you back on top of the building." That's not going to happen. However, what will happen is that you will find out that the law (the key word here is law) of gravity works every time for everyone. What goes up must come down. It is a law (made by God, not man) and it will not fail. The Bible says, "My people are destroyed for lack of knowledge. Because you have rejected knowledge, I also will reject you from being priest for Me; because you have forgotten the law of your God, I also will forget your children" (Hosea 4:6). Have you ever heard the saying **"ignorance of the law is no excuse?"** That simply means that just because you did not recognize the speed limit, you will still be given a ticket if you violate the speed limit. If you run a stop sign and a police officer sees you doing it, 99% of the time the officer will fine you for violating the law. However, if you violate God's law then 100% of the time you will deal with the repercussions of violating God's law. Because God's Law never fails!

Many people make the mistake of thinking that God's law isn't working because they don't always see the effect right away. That's because of God's mercy. God often gives us a chance to repent (to get it right, to turn 180 degrees and go the other way). That's why he is known as a loving God. Have you taken advantage of this gift and turned away from your sin? This is God's promise to us. Once we ask Jesus to come into our life and we make a mistake, this is what God promises: "If we confess our sins, He is faithful and just to forgive us our sins and to cleanse us from all unrighteousness" (I John 1:9). What a wonderful gift and it is ours for the asking. We need the spirit of God flowing in our lives in order to win this spiritual battle. This battle is against principalities, against powers, against the rulers of the darkness of this age, against spiritual hosts of wickedness in the heavenly places, even in our finances.

Remember that seducing spirits follow a path of destruction without reason. Every day we read in our newspapers or hear on our news broadcast about people doing what seems unimaginable.

Take for instance, lust. Why would a seemingly happily married man or woman with a wonderful family go out, get involved with another woman or man, and lose their family? Lose everything. Take for example, Senator Larry Craig from the State of Idaho, who pleaded not guilty to allegations of lewd conduct in a Minnesota airport public restroom. This story had dominated most major television stations as well as most major newspapers Roll Call, a Capitol Hill newspaper that first reported the case, said on its website Monday that "Craig was arrested June 11 by a plain clothes officer investigating complaints of lewd conduct in a men's restroom at the Minneapolis-St. Paul International Airport," By William M. Welch, USA TODAY. Here is a man who holds one of the highest and most powerful offices in the land but because of his actions his career and reputation has been greatly damaged. Not to mention the pain and disappointment of family, friends and colleagues."

Even our former president, President Bill Clinton who managed to stay in office for two terms had his presidency marred by his **scandal** with **Monica Lewinsky. He was accused of having an immoral sexual encounter with the** White House intern.

There are also several cases of female teachers having physical relationships with their students. Judith Wallace a charter schoolteacher was arrested in Maricopa County, Arizona on April 19, 2007 for sexual misconduct with a minor.

How about greed? Why would a seemingly successful business person that has been highly respected and honored for years in his or her community risk getting involved in illegal activities for a few dollars more? I remember a case in Newport News, Va. that involved a very successful real estate broker. His firm had been around for decades. At sixty-five years of age, this man was well- respected throughout the

Peninsula area. One day I read an article in the local paper about this same man having been arrested for his association with drug dealing.

Now, let's look at debt. *Wants* are rationalized as *needs*. It seeks a false pursuit of happiness that once obtained, usually leaves us empty and unfulfilled. We are a society that is constantly in the pursuit of happiness. After all, the Declaration of Independence says, "We hold these truths to be self-evident, that all men are created equal, that they are endowed by their Creator with certain unalienable Rights that among these are Life, Liberty and the pursuit of Happiness." **The Declaration of Independence of the Thirteen Colonies** in CONGRESS, July 4, 1776. There are two things here that we should pay close attention to. Number one: it says happiness and not joy. Number two what is joy? According to the American Dictionary of The English Language, by Noah Webster, 1828, the definition of Joy is to rejoice; to be glad; to exult; to give joy to congratulate, to entertain kindly. Happiness is defined as the agreeable sensations, which spring from the enjoyment of good; that state of being in which desires are gratified; positive pleasure or an excitement of agreeable sensations.

What all this means to me is this: Joy is an emotion deep within us. It is usually activated by love or an action that can be translated into love, such as an act of kindness, a gentle touch, a special word of encouragement. Joy is like the fire in a fireplace on a cold winter's night. When you cuddle up close to the fire with someone special and the flames have died down. The hot embers burn just the log and the flame glows simply for hours consistently at the same toasty warm temperature.

This is what happiness means to me: to be in a state of doing something I like a lot. Because happiness is based on what's happening such as if I am buying a new car, getting a promotion, watching the game (with my team winning) or going on vacation. Happiness often fades soon after the actual event has concluded. It's like working on a job and anticipating the next paid holiday for time off. Soon after the holiday is over, we forget what happened and start looking forward to the next holiday. We constantly seek the next event to try to recapture that feeling of happiness. This is called the pursuit of happiness.

When it comes to consumer debt, we often rationalize. I have done many financial workshops. One of the most common reasons I hear for owning a credit card is, "I only have a credit card for emergencies." I then ask, "When did Red Lobster or Applebee's become an emergency?" The Spirit of Debt, as always, helps us to rationalize and place importance on things that really are not important at all. It is a matter of choosing which voice to listen to, the voice of wisdom that says, "Why don't you wait on that, maybe you can work on it later" or "I need to talk to my spouse before I do this." Will you listen to the voice of instant gratification (the voice controlled by the Spirit of Debt) that says, "You'd better get it now because it will be gone. I love it; I just have to have it! I always wanted one of these!" or "I don't need any one telling me what to do. I am my own man or woman." The real battle is in your mind (I highly recommend a book by Joyce Meyer, titled The Battlefield of the Mind). Think about it. Whenever you have made an unwise decision, did you have a conversation going on in your head? That's because when you have Jesus in your life, the Holy Spirit is always there to guide us in the truth. People who don't know Jesus yet call this their conscience. How do you really know who's talking to you? Good question. Always remember this: The Holy Spirit leads us into all truth. A demonic spirit screams, "I've got to have it!" God's word says, "When he has brought out all his own, he goes on ahead of them, and his sheep follow him because they know his voice. But they will never follow a stranger; in fact, they will run away from him because they do not recognize a stranger's voice." (John 10:4–5). Whose voice have you been following?

Most consumer debt is a vile manifestation of Satan himself, conceived in the pit of Hell. Think about the examples I have given you. What did any of these people gain from their actions? They lost a great deal; not to mention the pain and dishonor to family and friends. When consumer debt rules, does it not bring pain and destruction? How many people have lost what took years of hard work to obtain because they listened to the wrong voice? They lost not only money but also their marriages, their health, families, and even businesses that have been in the family for years.

One day I was picking my son up from school. The father of one of his classmates came over to me and said, "Frank can I talk to you for a minute?"

"Sure," I said. "What's up?"

He said, "I understand you are teaching people about finances and managing debt."

"Yes," I said. "I am. I'm teaching classes at my church."

He said, "You know, I'm a clinical psychiatrist and in my practice I have been noticing a definite increase in the number of patients that are having debt related issues. I was hoping that you and I could have lunch one day and discuss this matter. I would like to seek a better understanding of how debt could be affecting my patients." I told him I would be glad to help in any way I could.

Another time a friend sent me an article he found on the web. This following is quoted from the article:

Killer Debt: Is your credit card making you sick? By Libby Wells, Bankrate.com: "The surest way to ruin a man who doesn't know how to handle money is to give him some." George Bernard Shaw, Heartbreak House

Never mind what a stack of overdue bills can do to your credit rating. The more important consideration might be how does being financially overextended affect your health? A study by Ohio State University suggests that people who are stressed about debt, particularly from credit cards, tend to be in worse physical condition than folks without money worries. Researchers found that the price of financial anxiety ranges from heart attacks, insomnia and explosive emotions to difficulty doing such simple tasks as climbing stairs and carrying groceries. And the people ailing the most are those with big chunks of their income tied up in credit card bills. "Debt-to-income ratio is significantly associated with higher levels of impairment," the study notes.

Debt stress and health linked

The link between debt stress and health was discovered by Paul J. Lavrakas, director of OSU's Center for Survey Research, and former colleague Patricia Drentea, who is now assistant professor of sociology at the University of Alabama-Birmingham. The results of their study --

a 1997 random telephone survey of more than 1,000 Ohioans -- were published in the February 2000 issue of "Social Science & Medicine." While it's well known that stress is detrimental, OSU's research is the first to show a connection between health and the strain of credit card debt. "For the individual consumer this is not a new message," acknowledges Lavrakas. "But what's striking is the risk you could be taking down the road with how you manage your debt. The pair focused on credit card debt because it's often an indicator of hardship. Families having a tough time making ends meet frequently turn to plastic to pay for basic necessities such as food, medicine, clothes and even the rent or mortgage. "Credit card debt may be a more sensitive barometer of financial well-being than income because it may tap into more long-term deprivation," they wrote.

What were the factors considered?

They considered factors such as the total amount of card debt and available credit, the number of cards used and whether participants carried a balance. The researchers also queried people on vital physical statistics, disabilities, smoking and drinking habits, job status, race and education. Even when common health barometers such as age were taken into account, debt stress appeared to play a role in participants' physical condition. Drentea says that people worrying about credit card bills were more likely to smoke and be overweight. In a 1999 follow-up survey, Lavrakas says many respondents reported heart problems. "Heart attack was the most prominent health problem we noted," he says. Second to that were sleeplessness, the inability to control emotions and a loss of concentration. (http://www.bankrate.com/brm/news/cc/20000410.asp)

CHAPTER 5

Retiring In an Ocean Of Red Ink

The golden years are supposed to be a time when we enjoy the fruits of our labor. It's supposed to be a time when you and your spouse get to do all the things you put off while raising you children. Things like vacations, a summer home, art collections, and travel. That sports car you always wanted and having the grand kids over with that wonderful option of sending them back home. A time to downsize to a smaller home, with less maintenance and of course, less yard to be mowed. A time when you finally get to burn your appointment book or throw out the PDA or Blackberry. When the only thing you need to make for dinner is reservations. When you can do what you really like doing and money is not a concern. The only alarm clock you need is the sunlight coming into your room and resting on your face, a time of appreciation and thanksgiving to God. Not to mention the good health to enjoy it all. You say to yourself, with a smile on your face, "This is why I've worked hard all my life. It is how I always dreamed it would be."

Unfortunately, this is not a reality for most of our retirees. For far too many of them, the dream has become a nightmare. Strapped with overwhelming debt and the high cost of health-care, many retirees have to make decisions between daily needs and medical needs. Many of our senior citizens are forced to sell their homes because of rising taxes or to downsize to a more affordable dwelling. They are forced to leave the home where they raised their children and maybe their grandchildren. All of their lifelong efforts and joyful memories stripped away because of the heavy burden of debt.

Many of our senior citizens live in unsafe neighborhoods because they cannot afford to move to a better community. Remembering the tree lined street where they used to take walks after dinner holding hands, the park a block away where they took their children and watched them play in the sandbox or pushed them on the swings. The children are all grown up now with families of their own. The neighborhood is drug infested, crime is rampant, and they are afraid to leave the house, prisoner in their own homes. This is too often a common scenario in so many of our major cities today.

Only 5% of our retirees live where they want, eat where they want, drive what they want and travel where they want. They are living the lifestyle that **95% of people who retire today have inadequate financial means: in layman's terms, they are broke.** they want. They are living the lifestyle that they always dreamed of living. On the other hand, 95% of people who retire today have inadequate financial means: in layman's terms, they are broke. What has caused such a disparity in the lives of our senior citizens? I believe the number one reason is the lack of financial education. The number two reason is consumer debt. When I was growing up, I was always told, "As long as you had a roof over your head, clothes on your back and food on the table then you'll be doing good." You must understand that the people who told me this loved me very much. They were giving me the best information that they had at the time. This was the formula they were given and they were living by it. If it was good enough for them, then why wouldn't it be good enough for me? What they didn't know was that this concept was great during the Great Depression. However, this concept is inadequate in today's economy. In today's economic system, you must have a plan for the future in order to enjoy the future.

I was also told to get a good education and get a good job. Once again, people who really loved me gave me sound advice, but the advice was not completely accurate. Again they were living on the presumption that if it was good enough for them, then why wouldn't it be good enough for me? The reality is that many people with great educations have ended up in financial ruin because they were not educated and disciplined with their personal finances. How many people have great jobs, some even have their own businesses, but are living from payday to payday?

There are so many examples today of people in ridiculous financial conditions. I was reading a book once on creating wealth and the author told a story of a woman who had been given an allowance of $250,000 a year for clothing. Now I know some women who wish they had an allowance like that. However, wait before you get too excited. This woman was barred from a very expensive boutique because she was behind in paying her clothing bill! A friend of mine, a financial adviser for a major airline, told me about people in his profession that make well over six figures. When the time came for them to retire, they could not afford to retire. The moral of this story is, just because you know how to make money does not mean that you know how to manage it.

> Just because you know how to make money does not mean that you know how to manage it.

The people who learned how to set goals in life (prepare a plan of action) and had been educated in how to manage their finances (budgeting and investing), are the people who ended up in the 5% category, living the lifestyle of their dreams. Remember "the rich get richer and the poor get poorer?" You can only truly teach what you know. I often ask this question, "What would you consider a good retirement package?" Most people would agree that 50% of their current salary and medical benefits would be a good retirement package. Then, I ask this question, "If you are struggling with the 100% of the salary that you are currently earning then how are you going to make it with 50% less in retirement?" Have you ever stopped and asked yourself that question? The truth of the matter is that most people do not retire with a generous retirement of 50% or more. Actually, it is much less.

Thirty years ago, one of the most important tools for retirement was to own your own home. Home ownership was a part of the American dream. It was not only a great place to raise a family but it also provided a source of cash flow for retirement. It was considered a vital asset that would be left to the children as a part of their inheritance. Home ownership had many options that would add to a family's wealth and for many families it was the only real asset they had to leave their children. This was done with the hope of giving their children a better start in life, something that they could build on and make a better life for their families. The Bible says, *"A good man leaves an inheritance for his children's children, but a sinner's wealth is stored up for the righteous."* (Proverbs 13:22)

When I first read this scripture, I thought what an awesome system God had given us. Let us examine what it is saying. A good man leaves an inheritance not for his children, but for his *children's* children. Take for example a man (or woman) who has managed his family's finances well (a good steward) and is only a few short years from retirement. Because he has been a good steward, at this stage in his life, his living expenses are minimal; his house is paid off or close to being paid off; the car(s) are paid for; he has no consumer debt (such as credit cards) and his income is at its highest.

Now, when are the cost of living expenses for a young family at its highest? Would you agree that it is when they are first starting out in life to build a future, to buy a new house, start a family, educate their family, and build their retirement plan? As a grandparent, what if you could say to your child, "Don't worry about the children's school clothes. We are going to buy them. We are going to give you the down payment for your house (it's our gift). We have already started an investment fund for the grandchildren's education." And, by the time they are ready for college; their tuition will be paid." Does this thought bring joy to your heart? Wait, because it gets better. Because of all the money you have saved your children, they have learned to be good stewards from your example. They will be able to duplicate what you did and do for their children what you have done for them. This will pass on from generation to generation. Is that an awesome system or what? Remember, the Bible says, "A good man leaves an inheritance for his children's children."

Satan has even devised a way to get the last resource a man has, to provide financial stability for his family later in life. In our culture, we love to rename things. That way it makes them more acceptable, even when we know they are wrong. In the Old Testament, a woman living with a man *that was not her husband* could be stoned to death. When I was growing up, we called a man and woman who were not married and living together, "living in sin." Today we call it "living-in." Teen pregnancy is at an all time high. The divorce rate is over sixty percent and the moral fabric of our society is rapidly eroding. You are probably saying, "What does that have to do with me?" Everything! I once heard a pastor say, "If you hang around the river bank long enough you will slip in."

To continue my point, less than thirty years ago, when a person took another loan out on their home in addition to the original loan, it was called a second mortgage. In order to qualify for a second mortgage, one would have to sit down with the bank's loan officer and prove their ability to pay back the loan. This was a tool usually used to start a new business, send a child to college, save a farmer from a bad harvest season, etc. It was used as a last ditch effort to save a family from financial disaster. It was almost never approved to eliminate consumer debt.

Credit cards and consumer debt had all but taken over our economy. There were so many people with maxed out credit cards, over the credit card limit and behind on their credit card payments, that bankruptcies were breaking new records. Now we have gone to equity loans that unlike their counterpart, (Second Mortgages), require little accountability in paying off the debt. That is because if you don't pay, you lose your home. The new tools for financial freedom include schemes such as equity loans and amortized rate mortgage loans (ARMS) where your mortgage fluctuates according to the interest rate and interest only loans. They have caused foreclosure rates to set new records with millions of people losing their homes. These new tools for financial freedom have millions of hard working everyday people, in financial bondage.

I remember about twenty-five years ago, when my wife and I moved from Hamden, Connecticut to Hampton, Virginia. A friend of mine had run into some very serious financial problems. He had a beautiful home. The first time I saw it I thought, "Man I wish I had a house like this." It was unique because the kitchen and den were upstairs and all the bedrooms were downstairs and located in a nice section of the city. My friend took out a second mortgage for about ten thousand dollars in an unconventional way because of his credit history. I don't think that the banks would have approved the loan. Within less than a year, my friend was unable to make the payments and the bank foreclosed on his home and took over the ownership of his house. My friend had lost his beautiful home that was worth about eighty thousand dollars. Now here is the kicker: he ended up renting the house back from the new owner for more than what he had been paying for his mortgage!

Always remember, you are going to have to live somewhere. We all have seen and heard the advertising for equity loans. They sound something like this, "Tired of those high interest credit card loans? Want to take that much-needed vacation? Tired of driving that old clunker? How about adding a new addition on to your home? Become debt free, pay off all your bills with a home equity loan from ACME." Can you possibly tell me how you can become debt free by borrowing more money? Do you recognize this voice -the Spirit of Debt? One of the best assets for retirement has now become a liability. At fifty-five years of age, how long did you think it would take to pay off that $50,000 loan?

In Deuteronomy 28:12, the Bible says, *"The LORD will open the heavens, the storehouse of his bounty, to send rain on your land in season and to bless all the work of your hands. You will lend too many nations but will borrow from none."* It has never been God's intention for his people to be in debt. Most people, Christian and non-Christian, have no idea that God even has a financial plan. Let's face it, in order to lend to another nation, it is going to take more than one dollar or that ten dollars you last placed in the offering plate at church feeling like you had just done God a big favor. The Bible says, **"Sowing Generously, Remember this: Whoever sows sparingly will also reap sparingly, and whoever sows generously will also reap generously." (2 Corinthians 9:6) This is how God's financial system works for those who trust him.**

CHAPTER 6

The Spirit of Debt Acceptable in the Church

E ven the church has fallen victim to the Spirit of Debt with little or no thought to what God's word says in Proverbs 22:7, "The rich rule over the poor and the borrower is servant to the lender."

Drugs and alcohol are not acceptable in the church but somehow debt is. Imagine this: On a Sunday morning, while you and your family are sitting in your favorite pew, a stranger walks in and sits down beside you. He reaches into his coat pocket, pulls out a flask filled with alcohol and begins to drink it. You would be appalled! If someone came into the church, pulled out a bag of marijuana, rolled a marijuana cigarette and began to smoke it, you would want the ushers to call the police and have him arrested. Maybe there is a member of your congregation you have known for many years. Your families have attended many social events together. On this particular Sunday, there had been a family dispute and your friend's wife was sitting next to you. What if her husband walked over to where you were sitting, grabbed his wife and began to verbally and physically abuse her? Would you not do everything in your power to stop the abuse? Would you also want to sever your relationship with her husband?

The above actions are not tolerated in the church. However, your friend can walk into the church on Sunday morning, sit down beside you and begin to tell you about all the great sales that were at the mall on Saturday. Your friend will also tell you how she overcharged on her credit cards. She'll even tell you how the cashier turned down two cards before she could find one that she could use, and you all laugh about it. *Drugs and alcohol are not acceptable in the church but debt is.* Remember the number one cause of divorce is money—the lack of money. In addition, debt is one of the main causes of drug and alcohol abuse.

Faith comes by hearing - and hearing by the word of God. After three decades of marketing, advertisers have convinced our society with the use of songs and commercials that instant gratification is the way. Here are a few examples that I believe have had a very powerful impact on how we think today: a song titled "It's Your Thing, Do What You Want to Do," by the Isley Brothers; a commercial for Burger King had the jingle, "Have it your way," and a song titled "What's Love Got to Do With it?" by Tina Turner. There was also a McDonalds' commercial, "You deserve a break today."

Do you remember the television show Fantasy Island? It was about a special island where people could go and have all their fantasies come true for a price. Today we spend millions of dollars mostly on credit cards trying to find our own fantasy island, but we've renamed it. We call it our Dream Vacation. After all, we deserve a break today don't we? Why can't I have it my way? It's my thing: I should be able to do what I want to do. In today's culture, many people's dream vacation is to get away from all the everyday responsibilities. That often means kids and spouses. Their idea of a dream vacation is to sit by the pool in a secluded resort with a good book or lie out on a tropical beach and watch the sunset. Maybe it's a fishing trip with the boys or that perfect round of golf by the Oceanside. After all, what's love got to do with it?

The concept here is, you can do whatever seems right to you, and no one has the right to tell you otherwise. Take that fantasy cruise and forget about your cares (they will be there when you get back to reality and so will the cost of the cruise). The Bible says, "In those days Israel had no king; all the people did whatever seemed right in their own eyes." Judges 21:25

No longer is it bad to be in Debt

We live in a *buy now and pay later* society. We want it fast and we want it now! No longer is it bad to be in debt. Sixty years ago, it was considered a flaw in your character not to pay your bills. In those days, when a man gave his word it was tied to his character. People would make very large financial commitments (covenant/promises) based on only a handshake to seal the deal. His word was backed by everything he stood for as a man. He would rather lose everything he had than go back on his word. Jesus said, "Heaven and earth will pass away, but my words will never pass away," (Matthew 24:35) This is the character of God. Where did you think we got it? My dad always taught me that a man is only as good as his word. **As a nation, we have turned away from this godly characteristic—the strength of character and integrity that made our nation great.**

We have adopted a new way of life called "politically correct." What does that mean? It means that what I say today might change tomorrow and even though I said it, I did not mean what I said (everyone does whatever seems right in his or her own eyes). What was done sixty years ago with a handshake, is done today with contracts as thick as phone books. A battery of lawyers oversees our decisions because our word is more like an ever-changing chameleon than it is a solid rock - a foundation we can rely upon.

Today debt is used as a status symbol. There use to be a slogan that represented the way of life in America: "baseball, apple pie and Chevrolet." Now the slogan would be baseball, apple pie and debt. We love to show off our new toys: cars, surround sound systems, laptops, play stations, clothes and jewelry. Not to mention the new hairstyles, some people pay hundreds of dollars for plaits. Excuse me, braids because when they were plaits they were free!

I once heard someone say, "The difference between men and boys are the price of their toys." Several decades of promoting instant gratification is woven into the very fabric of our society and has infiltrated the church. Satan has found a way to inhibit the church's mission (*Then Jesus came to them and said, "All authority in heaven and on earth has been given to me. Therefore, go and make disciples of all nations, baptizing them in the name of the Father and of the Son and of the Holy Spirit, and teaching them to obey everything I have commanded you. And surely I am with you always, to the very end of the age." (Matthew 28:18-20)* I believe that according to the word of God, there are two types of New Testament Saints. First, there are those who go; we call them missionaries. In reality, we are all missionaries in our own neighborhoods. The second types of

New Testament Saint are those who send; they are the people who are not called to go but who financially support those who are sent.

God prospers us (Christians, his children) that we may bless others and finance the gospel (But remember the LORD your God, for it is he who gives you the ability to produce wealth, and so confirms his covenant, which he swore to your forefathers, as it is today. Deuteronomy 8:18 God gives us the resources and he expects us to be disciples (disciplined followers of Christ) and get his word out.

Over three decades the church has been teaching faith, prosperity and how to live a life of abundance. This teaching has been wasted. Instead of using it for the end time harvest, we are using it for down payments and monthly payments. The party is over!

How much do we bring to God in tithes and offerings?

"Christian Retailing" ran an article by Ralph Rath many years ago, that said, "Christians spend less than an average of $2.17 per week on Christian related items including tithes and offerings." Notice that I said *bring* the tithe not *give* the tithe. The Bible says (A tithe of everything from the land, whether grain from the soil or fruit from the trees, belongs to the LORD; it is holy to the LORD, Leviticus 27:30). You can't give God what already belongs to him. However, you can return it to him. We will talk more on this later.

We want God to meet our needs: heal our bodies, protect our children, restore our marriages and bless our finances, all for $2.17 a week. Most Christians spend more on pizza than they do on the kingdom of God. When we go into a restaurant for dinner, we have already mentally prepared ourselves to leave a tip of at least 15%. I know people who would be embarrassed if you left less than 15% for the waitress or waiter. They would actually be ashamed to go back, for fear of what someone might think.

How much do we pay in taxes? The average tax bracket is 28% to 33%. When we see that deduction from our paychecks, we just say, "Oh well, everyone has to pay taxes." Yet when it comes to the things of God, we give God less than a tip. The same God we cry out to for the healing of our bodies, protection of our children, restoration of our marriage and blessing of our finances. When was the last time you received a miracle or healing from Pizza Hut or Red Lobster? Isn't it amazing that we care more about what people think, than we care about what God thinks?

Why do we think this way? Since the Garden of Eden, Satan has been deceiving people about church, God and money (God's portion). Before we can walk in victory concerning our finances or any other area of life, we must examine the truth and cast out the lie.

All the preacher wants is your money!

All the preacher wants is your money. How often have you heard this statement before? Maybe you have made the statement yourself. I know that I made it before I found out the truth, because I knew very little about church and nothing about God having a financial plan. All I ever heard about the church and money was how much the church needed. I heard people talk about what kind of car the pastor had, the type of house he owned, the neighborhood he lived in and where his kids went to school. I never gave a second thought to it being a lie until I read a book called **War on Debt**. And now I challenge you to examine why you believe this lie, that all the preacher wants is your money.

Why not say, "All the local grocery store wants is your money." Have you ever walked in to your local grocery store and filled up your shopping cart with everything that you needed then headed to the door, waved good-bye to the store clerk or the store manager and walked out of the store without paying? Of course not! Wrong! If you had even attempted something like that, you would have probably been on the six o'clock news. However, we don't say, "All the Grocer wants is our money."

How about your local banker? All he wants is to see you debt free, right? That's why we say, "The bank gave us the loan." We forget about that hour or two we sat there signing away everything we had in case we don't make the payments as promised. I know the banker just gave you that $100,000 and you just smiled and said good-bye. Right? Wrong again! When you leave the bank, you have mortgaged everything including your children. But we don't say, "All the Banker wants is your money."

The car dealer only cares that you have the best means of transportation, right? The insurance sales representative, the realtor, the doctor, hospitals, HMO's and the fast food chains are all only concerned about you. Isn't that great? Then why don't they call up the unemployment office and tell them about these benefits: after all, they don't want your money! How many times have we read in the paper or seen on the news about fraud in major corporations (remember Savings & Loan scams) in the nineties and more recently the Enron corporations disaster? In both cases, people lost millions if not billions of dollars because of deceitful and illegal operations. Operations that made a few people very rich and made many people lose their life savings. People have been subjected to false documents, false investments, junk bonds and stolen pension funds. People called the next day looking for companies to invest in. Wall Street is still setting new records. I haven't heard anyone say, "All they want is your money."

Isn't it interesting that out of all these different people and professions, the only one that "wants your money" is the Preacher? If you really think these other professionals care about you, then try calling them up at 2:00 am and ask them to pray for your sick child. Ask them to come and encourage you when your doctor tells you that he has found cancer in your body. Will they be there when your spouse walks out on you after twenty years of marriage? But remember, all the preacher wants is our money.

I am not deceived nor I am I naïve. I know that there are people out there that are in the office of a pastor that don't handle money properly. In fact, let me cut to the chase. I have been straightforward with you up to this point and I don't intend to stop now! Some people in the office of a pastor are robbing people. They are doing it in the name of the Lord.

I want to try to bring clarity to this issue once and for all. There is a big difference between a man who impregnates his wife and a man who becomes a father. A father is going to love, protect, encourage and provide for his children. A male will tell you about his children but he will not invest himself in their lives. (This reminds me of the saying – *Anyone can be a father; it takes someone special to be a dad*). That's why it is said, "Just because you're a male, it does not make you a man." The same thing applies to a pastor. Just because you stand in the pulpit does not make you a pastor. The true definition of Pastor is to be a shepherd. Jesus has set the standard.

There are many more good Shepherds (Pastors) then there are mislead Shepherds. I don't want what happened to me to happen to you. When I was a young man in my twenties, I knew of a pastor that was having an affair with the neighbor's wife in the apartment complex where I lived. When her husband was out to sea, the pastor would come to visit her during the week. I wasn't saved (I had not accepted Christ as my Lord and Savior) at the time. I thought, "Why should I go to church when the only difference between me and him is that he goes to church"? For many years, I would not have anything to do with any church because of this one man. God's love for me was so awesome because I had been involved in several situations that could have cost me my life. I could have died and gone to hell for eternity because I hadn't accepted Jesus in my life.

Many years later after I was saved, I heard Pastor Fred Price say, "A Pastor must live by the word of God just like you do. When a Pastor is in the pulpit, he is anointed by God but once he steps out of the pulpit, he has to make decisions like everyone else." Then I understood why that Pastor had done what he did so many years before. The Pastor had a gift from God to preach the word of God but he had not made the choice to practice the word in his personal life. I once heard a Pastor say, "Your gift (talent) can take you places that your character can't keep you." The moral of this story is, don't let what other people do keep you from all that God has for you. It has been over thirty years since that time. I can only think of a hand full of pastors that have fallen into sin. I think that record speaks for itself, don't you?

This is a Plot from Hell; Satan's Headquarters:

This is a plot from hell by Satan designed to destroy the people's trust in the integrity of the man of God (the Pastor). It is Satan's plot to deceive us into believing that all the preacher wants is our money. **That way, Satan can block the manifestation of God's power and prosperity in our lives.**

But beware, Satan wants to deceive us into believing this and once we accept it as the truth, then God can't bring us out of lack and poverty. The moment we accept this lie, we (not God) cancel out God's power to perform miracles on our behalf. You might say, "I don't believe that. He is God, He can do anything." The Bible says that God can't do anything. One thing God can't do is lie.

The Bible also says, "Now it came to pass, when Jesus had finished these parables, that He departed from there. When He had come to His own country, He taught them in their synagogue, so that they were astonished and said, "Where did this Man get this wisdom and these mighty works? Is this not the carpenter's son? Is not His mother called Mary? And His brothers James, Joses, Simon, and Judas? And His sisters, are they not all with us? Where then did this Man get all these things?" So they were offended at Him.

But Jesus said to them, "A prophet is not without honor except in his own country and in his own house." Now He did not do many mighty works there because of their unbelief." (Matthew 13:53-58 NKJ) Notice the scripture did not say that he did not *want* to do many mighty works. The Bible says "And he did not do many mighty works there because of their unbelief." Think about it: this was the hometown of Jesus. In other words, it was like a homecoming. If he wanted to heal anybody, wouldn't you think it would have been the people that he grew up with?

Don't get religious on me now! Jesus was a real person. Imagine if you went back to your hometown as a multi-billionaire and most of the people you loved and cherished were still there. You could take care of all of their needs from your reserve fund. You mean to tell me that you would not do it? You would leave them broke and sick and just drive away? I don't think so.

That's why Satan wants us to believe this lie, so we won't receive our miracle either. The Bible says "And without faith it is impossible to please God, because anyone who comes to him must believe that he exists and that he rewards those who earnestly seek him." (Hebrews 11:6) I love what the Word tells us in this verse. The word does not say because I don't go to church enough, I don't pray enough, I don't sing enough, I don't give enough or I don't go to enough Joyce Meyer conferences. It says without faith. My faith is the only thing that really pleases God. All of the other things I mentioned are good, but without faith, it does not please God.

What does it mean to have faith? Another word we can use is trusting God. Take this for example: How would you know if your children had faith that you will pick them up from school? You would only know when you arrived and saw your children standing at the designated place, waiting for you to pick them up (Faith). Then you would know by their actions that they have trusted in you.

Now look at another part of this scripture: it also says, "And that he rewards those who earnestly seek him." What does this really mean? Many times, I hear Christians talk about God meeting our needs. There is a culture in the church that believes that God only gives us what we need. According to this scripture that is not true, because it says "That God rewards those who earnestly (another translation) and diligently seek him."

First, why don't we define reward? According to Webster's New Collegiate Dictionary, something as money given or offered for a special service, as a return of a lost article; rewarding offering or likely to offer satisfaction or gratification. What if I told you that I needed twenty dollars and you told me that you would pay me twenty dollars if I helped you put a shed up in your back yard? When we completed the shed, you gave me twenty dollars. Have you rewarded me? No, you have just paid me what you owed me. If you had given me a hundred dollars then you have gone beyond my need. You were so pleased with the work I had done, that you decided to give me an additional eighty dollars as a bonus (reward). Just to show your appreciation for my excellent work you have given me much more than we agreed upon. The extra eighty dollars was not expected because I had agreed to do the job for twenty dollars. The eighty dollars is beyond my expectation or need, that's why I consider it a reward. When we seek God diligently, He gives us much more than we deserve, expect or need because God rewards faithfulness.

This I believe is the bottom-line and the reason Satan wants us to believe the lie about Pastors and how many have been deceived: The Bible says "So they rose early in the morning and went out into the Wilderness of Tekoa; and as they went out, Jehoshaphat stood and said, 'Hear me, O Judah and you inhabitants of Jerusalem: Believe in the LORD your God, and you shall be established; believe His prophets, and you shall prosper.'" (2 Chronicles 20:20 NKJ). Many people believe in God and not his prophets (in those days they were the Pastors). They think that only God is going to bless them. Here God lays out his process of being blessed or successful: *believe in God and be established that your faith in God can not be moved.* According to Webster's New Collegiate Dictionary, established means, "to make secure or firm. Then it says "To believe in his prophets and you shall prosper." This is where most people drop their candy in the mud.

They believe in God but because they can see the prophet is not perfect like Jesus, their belief waivers. They allow Satan to drop little bombs in their minds. "You see? He walked right pass you and didn't speak." " He called Sister Barnes and asked her to be on the committee and forgot about you." We take offense, our belief system becomes damaged and our ability to prosper has been disconnected. What was that? Did I hear you say, you don't believe that? Let's look at it in a more direct point of view—there are always two sides to every coin. **Believe His prophets, and you shall prosper. Don't believe in his prophets and you won't!** Therefore, in reality, whether you prosper or not is not up to God nor is it up to Satan. The person in control is really you! Remember, whose voice will you listen to? Jesus said, "My sheep know my voice and another they will not follow."

Satan has limited power. Either many people overestimate Satan's power or they underestimate his power. Satan has three main methods he uses to attack us. They are to tempt us, accuse us and deceive us and the strongest of the three is deception. The battleground is usually located in the same place, between our two ears. This is called the battlefield of the mind. This is where we are attacked and our thoughts are bombarded with all sorts of things that confuse us. If left unchecked they will take us places and cause us to do things that we wish we had never done. The Bible says, *"Let no one say when he is tempted, I am tempted by God; for God cannot be tempted by evil, nor does He Himself tempt anyone. But each one is tempted when he is drawn away by his own desires and enticed. Then, when desire has conceived, it gives birth to sin; and sin, when it is full-grown, brings forth death."* (James 1:13-15)

As you can see, nothing *"just happens."* There is always a process, but if we don't understand the process, it can do us a great deal of harm. Let's examine the process: *(1) when desire is first conceived.* Let's say you see a new car and you really want it, so you talk to your spouse about it. You tell your spouse about the great price but you don't tell your spouse that it has a 28% interest-rate with a large balloon payment at the end. *(2) It gives birth to sin.* When your spouse asks you about the interest rate and the terms of payment you say, "It's the best rate he had." But you did not reveal that it was the best rate he had for you because your credit rating was so bad. You allowed your spouse to think that the rate was a lot lower than it was. *(3) "When it is full-grown it brings forth death."* Now you have signed the papers and brought the car home. Several months later, you're struggling financially and your spouse wants to know what's going wrong. Why are our bills so far behind? Why is the mortgage company threatening to foreclose on our house? Then you finally admit that you lied about being able to afford that new car, you thought you were getting a promotion and the boss had just announced unlimited overtime for the next year. You thought that you could make the payments with no problem (at least that's what the voice in your head told you). The promotion never happened, the overtime was cancelled and you deceived your spouse and now you are in financial ruin. You're going to lose everything and your spouse wants a divorce (the death of a marriage). **Sin will always take you further than you want to go, make you stay longer than you want to stay and make you pay more than you ever wanted to pay!**

This is an example of how the power of deception has destroyed the lives of many people. Deception is always mixed with the truth. It all started in the Garden of Eden when the serpent confronted Eve. The Bible says, "Now the serpent was more cunning than any beast of the field which the LORD God had made. And he said to the woman, "Has God indeed said, 'You shall not eat of every tree of the garden?" (Genesis 3:1)

I often say this to people: "If you walk out into your backyard and step into dog poop that was a mistake. Later if you walk back out into your backyard and step into the same pile of dog poop again you weren't deceived, you were just stupid! Stupid because you knew it was there and you made no effort to correct your actions. *Deception takes place when you don't know what's happening. If you know it's going to happen, it's not deception. The reality is that we make choices.*

Prosperity has been taught throughout the Bible "The thief does not come except to steal, and to kill, and to destroy. I have come that they may have life, and that they may have it more abundantly" (John 10:10). Why then does the body of Christ not have life more abundantly as according to the Bible? The Bible tells us that we can live a life with no lack in any area of our life. I know some of your minds have just responded like a pinball machine when you shake it too hard, it goes tilt. That means game over, I can't process anymore.

We read it and quote it all the time but never really understanding what it means. Most people know it as the **Shepherd's** prayer, "The Lord is my shepherd, I shall not be in want. He makes me lie down in green pastures, he leads me beside quiet waters" (Psalms 23:1-2, NIV). It says I shall not be in want! But there is a condition tied to this promise. The condition is, when the Lord is my shepherd. A shepherd leads, guides, provides and protects his sheep.

The second part says that he also makes us lie down in green pastures and leads us beside the still waters. Here is a picture of peace and serenity, **something most of us spend all our adult lives trying to obtain.** When you are living a life that is pleasing to God (following his word), all your needs are taken care of and you have found peace and purpose in your life. What is more fulfilling than that? I believe this is a glimpse of the abundance that God's word refers to.

Could it be because Satan has infiltrated people's minds and deceived them into believing the lie about Pastors and money? In most churches today, people don't want to hear the preacher talking about money. It doesn't matter how seldom he talks about money, most people feel that it is too often. This has intimidated the man of God and Satan is having his way in the pulpit!

Maybe this is the reason why, when the pastor does an altar call for financial needs the line is usually longer than for any other need in the church ("For faith comes by hearing and hearing by the word of God"). God's word says if the Pastor doesn't preach about it then we won't have the faith to receive it. We will continue to let Satan hinder God's prosperity in our lives and hinder the mission of the church; "And Jesus came and spoke to them, saying, "All authority has been given to Me in heaven and on earth. Go therefore and make disciples of all the nations, baptizing them in the name of the Father and of the Son and of the Holy Spirit, teaching them to observe all things that I have commanded you; and lo, I am with you always, even to the end of the age." Amen (Matthew 28:18-20) News flash: You are the church (The body of Christ).

Your pastor is a valuable asset.

Did you know that your pastor is a valuable asset? Most pastors could be top managers and CEO's receiving a very large salary. Do you really believe that it is your money that keeps your pastor preaching the word of God? Your pastor is being obedient to the call of God on his or her life. Remember God called them, not you! **His rewards and blessings are given by God**

> So Jesus answered and said, "Assuredly, I say to you, there is no one who has left house or brothers or sisters or father or mother or wife or children or lands, for My sake and the gospel's, who shall not receive a hundredfold now in this time—houses and brothers and sisters and mothers and children and lands, with persecutions—and in the age to come, eternal life." (Mark 10:29-30)

The reward for obeying God is never dependant on man; however, God will use men to bless other men. The reason the Pastor teaches you God's word concerning your finances is so you may receive all that God has planned for you to have ("For I know the plans I have for you," declares the LORD, "plans to prosper you and not to harm you, plans to give you hope and a future. Then you will call upon me and come and pray to me, and I will listen to you. You will seek me and find me when you seek me with all your heart." (Jeremiah 29:11-13) Satan wants to destroy our ability to walk in the love, peace, joy, divine health and prosperity that was purchased at the cross of Calvary by Jesus' death and resurrection.

Whenever anyone (not just the Pastor) decides to surrender their lives to the Lord (giving Jesus total control and live according to his word) we receive power from within (the Holy Spirit comes and lives inside of us). In other words, we now have the ability to live a life that is pleasing to God. Without accepting the gift of salvation (Jesus), we could never overcome the effects of sin (poverty, sickness, loneliness depression and a host of others). With Jesus as commander and chief of our lives, we can now become everything that God created us to be (this is a process; it is not an overnight event). How many years did it take you to mess up your life? Do you think it will be worth it to spend some time learning how to live in victory (love, peace, joy) regardless of your circumstance. Living a life filled with passion and purpose! Jesus promised that whatever you give up for his sake and the Gospel, you will receive a return on your investment of thirty, sixty, one hundred-fold in this life and eternal life. **Can you say what a deal!** Can your banker or financial planner make you that guarantee?

CHAPTER 7

The Double Minded Man

There is also the deception of how we see Jesus and money. What has been the message over the years about money and Jesus? When it comes to money and Jesus, we are very doubled minded. Therefore, when it comes to money and the church, we are also doubled minded.

The Pastor, Elder or a Deacon walks up to the pulpit and says, "You know that the things of this world will pass away and that's why we don't care about things. We don't need a lot of money, fortune or fame. All we need is Jesus, Amen." Then they will pray and say, "Now the ushers may take up the offering." Is there any wonder why most people are confused today? The Bible says, "If any of you lacks wisdom, he should ask God, who gives generously to all without finding fault, and it will be given to him. But when he asks, he must believe and not doubt, because he who doubts is like a wave of the sea, blown and tossed by the wind. That man should not think he will receive anything from the Lord; he is a double-minded man, unstable in all he does." (James 1:5-7). Based on this scripture, if we can't make up our minds then we cannot receive anything from God. That means no spiritual, physical, mental or financial healings.

That's why I believe it is so important that we know the truth, so our prayers won't be hindered. The Bible says "And you shall know the truth, and the truth shall make you free" (John 8:32). When most Christians are asked if they want to be like Jesus, the answer is always a resounding "Yes!" Then my question to you is what was Jesus like concerning money and prosperity? What was his financial statement?

Was he rich or was he poor? Did he live in poverty, lack, or a life of abundance? How did he live?

I want to share with you the facts that I have found and let you be the judge. Is that ok? Because the only thing that will, set you free is the truth that you know. Jesus said, "You will know the truth and the truth will make you free!"

December 25th is one of the holiest scenes of our time and celebrated around the world, yet it reeks of poverty. We know it as the Nativity Scene. This scene is recreated in many different languages through plays and dramas all over the world. Cards are sent all over the world in many different languages. Many people have the Nativity Scene in their homes and on their lawns. Even our churches would seem out of character if they did not display the Nativity Scene during the Christmas season.

Most of the things that we know about Jesus are surrounded by poverty. Joseph had his pregnant wife Mary (mother of Jesus) riding on a donkey. He couldn't find room in the inn, they stayed in a stable (with smelly animals) and Jesus was born in that stable. Poor Jesus!

Based on our culture today, if we were honest about how we felt, we would think to ourselves what a poor, awful existence! In other words, what if a psychiatrist showed you a picture of the Nativity Scene and said, "Tell me - what is the first thought that comes to your mind about their financial status?" What would be your answer? Don't get religious on me now! Just tell the truth. This is why the Bible tells us to renew our minds, "Do not conform any longer to the pattern of this world, but be transformed by the renewing of your mind. Then you will be able to test and approve what God's will is—his good, pleasing and perfect will" (Romans 12:2). Therefore, we can see the truth through God's eyes.

The lie of poverty surrounds what we know about Jesus, so let's examine the facts. Why were Joseph and Mary going to Bethlehem in the first place? The Bible says to register in the census that had been decreed in those days by Caesar Augustus. He issued a decree that a census should be taken of the entire Roman Empire. We see Mary riding on a donkey as being poor Mary. We fail to understand that during that time, a donkey was a valued means of travel. Today it would represent a Lexus or a Mercedes Benz. In that time, most people walked to their destination.

Why did Mary and Joseph sleep in the stable? Was it because they could not afford a room? No. The Bible says that there was no room in the inn, in other words it was booked. Think about it, if your wife was pregnant and she was having contractions, would she say to you, "Honey, let's ride about another hundred miles so we can find a place to stay." I don't think so and neither do you. The Bible says, "While they were there, the time came for the baby to be born, and she gave birth to her firstborn, a son. She wrapped him in cloths and placed him in a manger, because there was no room for them in the inn" (Luke 2:6–7). They couldn't just go a few blocks to the next available Holiday Inn.

One of the major deceptions in the Nativity Scene is the three wise men or Magi standing over the baby Jesus in the manger. Although it makes for a good picture, it is not a picture of truth. As long as we believe the Wise men were at the manger, we will miss the key events when they really found the child Jesus about two years later.

Let's read what the Bible says and then examine the facts:

"And there were shepherds living out in the fields nearby, keeping watch over their flocks at night. An angel of the Lord appeared to them, and the glory of the Lord shone around them, and they were terrified. But the angel said to them, "Do not be afraid. I bring you good news of great joy that will be for all the people. Today in the town of David a Savior has been born to you; he is Christ the Lord. This will be a sign to you: You will find a baby wrapped in cloths and lying in a manger. "Suddenly a great company of the heavenly host appeared with the angel, praising God and saying, "Glory to God in the highest, and on earth peace to men on whom his favor rests. "When the angels had left them and gone into heaven, the shepherds said to one another, "Let's go to Bethlehem and see this thing that has happened, which the Lord has told us about." So they hurried off and found Mary and Joseph, and the baby, who was lying in the manger. When they had seen him, they spread the word concerning what had been told them about this child, and all who heard it were amazed at what the shepherds said to them." (Luke 2:8–18)

As you can see, the Shepherds never mention the wise men in their account. They were not mentioned because they were not there.

Now let's find out when the Wise men or Magi actually found

the child Jesus. First, let's take a look at the Wise men themselves. Who were they? How many were there? Where did they come from? Why did they come? The Bible says, "After Jesus was born in Bethlehem in Judea, during the time of King Herod, Magi from the east came to Jerusalem and asked, 'Where is the one who has been born king of the Jews? We saw his star in the east and have come to worship him.' When King Herod heard this he was disturbed, and all Jerusalem with him. When he had called together all the people's chief priests and teachers of the law, he asked them where the Christ was to be born. 'In Bethlehem in Judea,' they replied, 'for this is what the prophet has written: But you Bethlehem, in the land of Judah, are by no means least among the rulers of Judah; for out of you will come a ruler who will be the shepherd of my people Israel.' Then Herod called the Magi secretly and found out from them the exact time the star had appeared. He sent them to Bethlehem and said, 'Go and make a careful search for the child. As soon as you find him, report to me, so that I too may go and worship him." (Matthew 2:1–8)

Why was King Herod so interested in the wise men's search for the Messiah? The Jewish people had been waiting for the Messiah for centuries - what made their search so different? There was a prophecy that said, "The ruler would come out of Bethlehem." What got Herod's attention was the arrival of the Wise men in Jerusalem.

How many times have we seen the pictures of three wise men traveling, either in a movie, on a Christmas card, in a book and especially in the actual Nativity Scene? We always see a picture of three men riding on a camel, each man has a neatly wrapped gift in his hand as though they had just left Macy's following a star. Where in the

Bible does it say that there were three wise men? The Bible says there were gifts of gold, Frankincense and myrrh. We translated that into one package per person and made three out of it, not so in the Bible.

When I was growing up, I loved to watch the old Roman movies, especially those that had Hercules, Samson or the gladiators as the theme. In those days, when one King would go to visit another Kingdom, he would always take many gifts. This was a *tribute* to honor the King. I remember in the movies there would be trunks of silver and gold, fine linens, perfumes and fine oils. There was a large caravan that would transport these items. They also had armed guards or soldiers to protect them from thieves during their travels. Many times people would be robbed in their travels and that's why it was customary for a caravan to be heavily guarded. This is why I believe that when Herod heard that this caravan fit for a King was in his kingdom and they weren't there to see him, he wanted to know why they were there. Think about it, what if you came home and found about fifty people in your house unexpectedly. What would be the first thing you'd want to know? "What are you doing here?"

Then the Bible says; "When they heard the king, they departed; and behold, the star which they had seen in the East went before them, till it came and stood over where the young Child was. When they saw the star, they rejoiced with exceedingly great joy. And when they had come into the house, they saw the young Child with Mary His mother, and fell down and worshiped Him. And when they had opened their treasures, they presented gifts to Him: gold, frankincense, and myrrh. Then, being divinely warned in a dream that they should not return to Herod, they departed for their own country another way" (Matthew 2:9–12, NKJ). The wise men continued on their journey and when the star stood over the house (not stable) where the young child (not baby) was they rejoiced with exceedingly great joy. They saw the young child (Jesus) with his mother Mary; they opened up their treasurers (checkbooks) and worshiped him. They presented him with gold, frankincense and myrrh.

Jesus has His ministry financed by the Wise Men!

When God calls us, he prepares us. When God orders it, he will pay for it! When the wise men opened their treasures to Jesus, he was too young to handle the gifts that were being presented. So what happened to the money?

First, we must understand more about Joseph whom Mary married. First of all Joseph was a carpenter (that's why they called Jesus the carpenter's son). Now in our society, when you think about a carpenter, what is the first thing that comes to your mind? How about handyman, someone who fixes stuff, installs cabinets, builds decks or maybe builds frames for houses? We consider him a blue-collar worker. We don't associate wealth with being a carpenter, although being a carpenter today will provide a very good living. We don't associate it with wealth or financial freedom. In Joseph's day, the carpenter often designed and built everything from the foundation to the roof. We call them architects today! Now we get a whole new picture. How many broke architects do you know? In other words, Joseph wasn't broke but had a very successful trade or vocation. With this in mind, I want to put you in Joseph's position.

Let's say that you had a two year old son. You loved and worshiped God and obeyed his word. One day Bill Gates, the president for Bank of America and Warren Buffet all came to your house. When you opened the door, they said that they heard you had a very special child and they wanted to leave him a gift. Then they each left you a cashier's check for one hundred million dollars. What would you do with the money? The Bible says, "When they had gone, an angel of the Lord appeared to Joseph in a dream. Get up," he said, "take the child and his mother and escape to Egypt. Stay there until I tell you, for Herod is going to search for the child to kill him." So he got up, took the child and his mother during the night and left for Egypt, where he stayed until the death of Herod. And so was fulfilled what the Lord had said through the prophet: "Out of Egypt I called my son. "When Herod realized that he had been outwitted by the Magi, he was furious, and he gave orders to kill all the boys in Bethlehem and its vicinity who were two years old and under, in accordance with the time he had learned from the Magi." (Matthew 2:13–16)

I always wondered why Herod killed every male child two years and younger. The Wise men (Magi) told him that they had been following the star in search of the Messiah about two years. Herod believe if he killed every male child two years and younger that he could not fail to kill the Messiah. This also proves again that when the Wise men finally found Jesus he was about two years old. That's why the Bible says, "When they found the young child," the toddler—not a baby.

I wanted to show you that just because we read things, see things or do things, doesn't mean they are true. We need to verify them through God's word (the Bible). What is tradition and what is truth are often like a blue shell crab in the Chesapeake Bay. When a crab sheds its hard shell for a period of time the crab's entire body is soft and we call it a soft shell crab (very delicious I might add). If you were to walk along the shore and see the crab's shell lying in the water, you can very easily mistake it for a real blue shell crab. But the moment you pick it up to examine it, you notice that it has no substance and no life in it. Even though it looks just like the real thing. This can be like religion! **Having knowledge of God but having no real substance.**

Many times in Christianity, we portray Jesus and the Apostles as being broke. Okay we don't come right out and say broke, we use terms like; in great need or not having their needs met. Where does sayings such as "poor as a church mouse" come from? When I look in the Bible, I don't find anything to substantiate these sayings. The Bible says, "When Jesus had called the Twelve together, he gave them power and authority to drive out all demons and to cure diseases, and he sent them out to preach the kingdom of God and to heal the sick. He told them: "Take nothing for the journey—no staff, no bag, no bread, no money, no extra tunic" (Luke 9:1–4). We must ask ourselves a very obvious question. Why do you have to tell broke people not to bring money? The answer is you don't. Jesus was teaching them to operate in faith. He wanted them to learn how to trust in God's provision and not on what they or the system could provide. The Spirit of Debt is destroying many lives and that's why this lesson is still needed in the church today. Rather than trusting God's system to provide for us, we run to the world's system.

Now let's look at this, "Then Jesus asked them, "When I sent you without purse, bag or sandals, did you lack anything?" "Nothing," they answered" (Luke 22:35). When they trusted in God's financial system, the Bible says that they lacked nothing. What does that mean? It means all their financial needs had been taken care of. The reason I spelled this out is because we can believe God for a physical or emotional healing, but when it comes to money somehow our belief system develops a major short. It begins to static like an old AM radio.

I believe that this is the key to fulfilling the Great Commission, if you can let the truth I am about to share into your heart and act on it. The Bible says, "All the believers were one in heart and mind. No one claimed that any of his possessions was his own, but they shared everything they had. With great power, the apostles continued to testify to the resurrection of the Lord Jesus, and much grace was upon them all. There were no needy persons among them. For from time to time those who owned lands or houses sold them, brought the money from the sales and put it at the apostles' feet, and it was distributed to anyone as he had need" (Acts 4:32-35). When most people read this, the first thing they think is what do I have to give up. We are so blinded with self that we don't see the power and blessings just pouring out of these words. First, they agreed. Second, they shared everything. Third, there was great power among them. Fourth, there were no needy persons among them. Among who? Them that shared. Fifth, some owned land, Sixth and some owned houses. They were real estate investors and landlords. This is where most people are hung up, thinking that it was their own personal dwellings that were sold and they ended up homeless. We fail to realize how God had already provided them with the means and it was their Love for God and the act of obedience to return it to God for his use.

What do you think God did for those people who obeyed him in this manner? The Bible says, "Give and it will be given to you: good measure, pressed down, shaken together, and running over will be put into your bosom. For with the same measure that you use, it will be measured back to you" (Luke 6:38). Seventh, the Apostles were able to take care of everyone who was in need. Notice what it did not say, that everyone was in need. That was an awesome financial system, don't you agree?

The story of Judas stealing the money from the disciples often overshadows his position in the ministry of Jesus. Judas was in charge of the money. Why did Jesus need someone in charge of the money? I don't know about you but I don't carry around enough money that I would need to place someone in charge of it. After all, Jesus had a businessman, Peter, the fisherman, and Matthew was a tax collector. I think any of those guys could have managed petty cash, don't you? Then why was Judas assigned to manage the money? The Bible doesn't say why but it does give us an idea of how much money was under Judas's control. Most of us know the story of Jesus feeding the five thousand people with only five loaves of bread and two fish. We know that feeding that many people with so little was truly a miracle; in fact, it was so awesome that most of the story is never told. The Bible says, "Late in the afternoon the Twelve came to him and said, "Send the crowd away so they can go to the surrounding villages and countryside and find food and lodging, because we are in a remote place here." He replied, "You give them something to eat. They answered, "We have only five loaves of bread and two fish—unless we go and buy food for all this crowd." About five thousand men were there (Luke 9:12–13).

The part that often gets omitted is when one of the disciples asked ,if they should go buy food for all the people? Why would that question even come into the picture unless they had the means to buy food for them? Think about it. One day you pull up to your driveway after a long day at work. All you want is a hot shower and a hot meal. When you arrive at your home, you see about one hundred of your friends and relatives standing in your driveway. When you ask them what was going on they say they were told to come to your place for a dinner party. Would you have enough money on you to go and provide food for everyone?

You see, Jesus didn't plan this either. He probably was just as surprised as you would have been (don't get religious on me now). He was the son of man as well as the son of God, because the Bible says that he often went off to rest. When you read the entire story, you will find that Jesus was trying to get away from the crowd and they followed him. That should provide more than enough evidence to show that he was not expecting to feed anyone. We also must take into account that there were more than five thousand people there that day, because when the disciples counted they only counted the men. They did not count the women and children (I will explain that to you later in the book). However, everyone had been provided for and there were precisely twelve baskets of food left over. The question must be asked, If Jesus had enough money to buy the food then why perform the miracle? I am glad you asked. I believe that Jesus used this opportunity to teach his disciples to trust in God's provision, more than just looking at what was in their hands (or in their bank account). It must have increased their faith to know that if God would provide for a crowd that size with so little, then he can do anything. As you can see, God's method can simply be providing you with the money. The miracle may be getting you to obey God when he prompts you to give it away for his purpose.

Why were the disciples so concerned about the rich getting into heaven? The Bible says, "Then Jesus said to his disciples, 'I tell you the truth, it is hard for a rich man to enter the kingdom of heaven. Again, I tell you, it is easier for a camel to go through the eye of a needle than for a rich man to enter the kingdom of God. "When the disciples heard this, they were greatly astonished and asked, "Who then can be saved?" Jesus looked at them and said, "With man this is impossible, but with God all things are possible" (Matthew 19:23–26). The disciples had possessions of their own and they were concerned that their possessions would hinder them from entering into the Kingdom of heaven.

Like most of the church today, we say that we don't want lots of money, fortune or fame because we are afraid it will keep us out of heaven. Then we pray to God to make our name great like He promised Abraham. *"God bless my business to overflowing."* Then we wonder why we are not seeing our prayers answered. We are doubled- minded. As the scripture says "unstable in all our ways." Think about it. There was Peter the fisherman and Matthew the tax collector, both business men. Remove your religious cloak and with a clear heart and a clear mind, answer this question. Does this sound like a broke bunch to you?

This is my last exhibit to prove my case that our Lord and Savior Jesus Christ was not poor. When Jesus was on the cross at Calvary, as he shed his precious blood for our sins something else was taking place. It was so important that it was recorded in the Bible during his execution. The Bible says, "When the soldiers crucified Jesus, they took his clothes, dividing them into four shares, one for each of them, with the undergarment remaining. This garment was seamless, woven in one piece from top to bottom. "Let's not tear it," they said to one another. "Let's decide by lot who will get it." This happened that the scripture might be fulfilled which said, "They divided my garments among them and cast lots for my clothing." So this is what the soldiers did (John 19:23-24). In the footnotes of my New International Version study Bible, it says that the garment that the guards gambled over was, "a type of shirt, reaching from the neck to the knees or ankles. Seamless, therefore too valuable to cut up" (John 19:23–24). In laymen's terms, it was a designer garment. This garment was without seam. I don't know of any clothing store where you can find a garment like this without seams hanging on their rack. It was so expensive that the guards did not want to tear it. These were Roman guards! Even they knew the value of it.

If I had simply said to you that Jesus wore expensive clothing, you would call me a heretic. I didn't just come in with the morning milk. I know there are some of you reading this that are calling me a heretic anyway. All I have to say to you is may the Holy Spirit bear witness to your spirit and bring light to this area, in Jesus' name, amen.

We must begin to see ourselves in Christ the way God sees us - especially in our finances. The Bible says, *"Beloved, I pray that you may prosper in all things and be in health, just as your soul prospers"* (3 John 1:2, NKJ). The truth of the matter is that we can't receive from God until we believe in God. The Bible says, "That if you confess with your mouth the Lord Jesus and believe in your heart that God has raised Him from the dead, you will be saved. For with the heart one believes unto righteousness and with the mouth confession is made unto salvation." If we expect to obtain anything from God, this is the process: whether it is healing, deliverance, forgiveness, finances or any other area of our life where we are expecting a move of God.

So when we say that we want to be like Jesus, we must know what Jesus was like in order to be like him. We can follow our religious beliefs and not know why we believe in them. Jesus often said, "According to your faith be it unto you," because what you truly believe is what you are going to have faith for (act on). For example, if you tell me to meet you at the train station at noon today and you will give me a thousand dollars, I'll say ok. When twelve noon comes, I will not be at the train station. Why? Because I did not believe you even though I said ok with my mouth. I did not believe in my heart. I will only act on that which I truly believe. If you continue to believe that Jesus lived in lack then you will act that way, however if you have gotten the revelation of your King and his Kingdom than you will act as an Ambassador of the King. Remember, "If any of you lacks wisdom, let him ask of God, who gives to all liberally and without reproach, and it will be given to him. But let him ask in faith, with no doubting, for he who doubts is like a wave of the sea driven and tossed by the wind. For let not that man suppose that he will receive anything from the Lord" (James 1:5-7). Because "But without faith it is impossible to please Him, for he who comes to God must believe that He is, and that He is a rewarder of those who diligently seek Him." (Hebrews 11:6)

> What you truly believe is what you are going to have faith for (act on).

Living in two worlds

As human beings, we live in two worlds. One world can be seen and is called the *natural* world. The other world cannot be seen and is called the *supernatural* or the *spiritual* world. You might say that you don't believe in the supernatural or the spiritual world, because you can't see it. If this is your argument, then you must stop breathing immediately because you can't see the air that sustains your life either. You can't see it but yet you depend on it (you believe it is there).

The things I have explained thus far have dealt primarily with the supernatural, the spiritual world, or the spiritual side of things. My main objective has been to expose the Spirit of Debt and how it works. Also, to deal with myths and lies that have held the church in captivity and hindered her in the world financially. We must also explore the natural world and how it has played a major part in our ability to accomplish all that God has set before us, especially in the area of finances. I will explain it this way, the supernatural or the spiritual world is God's part and the natural world is our part. I once heard a visiting Pastor say that he heard a Bible teacher say this: "I have some good news and I have some bad news. **The good news is that God will do his part. The bad news is he won't do yours.**" That's a good picture of how the supernatural and the natural world operates. In order to walk in victory we must obey God and do our part!

CHAPTER 8

The Connection between the Tithe and the Covenant

Before I can move into the second part of this book that I call the natural world, I must take the time to talk to you about one of the most important principles in the church today. Many people have different views about it, some agree, some don't. Some agree but still refuse to participate and some think it's a mute point and others just don't know. I believe that it is one of the most powerful parts of our walk with God. All that Jesus bought and paid for with his precious blood at Calvary is connected to our understanding of this principle. In order for us to fulfill the Great Commission, there must be a greater understanding of tithing.

I make no apologies for talking about tithing! I believe in tithing wholeheartedly! It is God's financial system and no man on earth or devil in hell is going to change that. I told you earlier that I am from the Blind Man's club (the one Jesus healed in the Bible). Once I was blind but now I see. If I go into the second part of this book and omit sharing with you about tithing, then I have just wasted your valuable time. Because you have read this far, I know that the Holy Spirit has revealed truth to your heart. I would not dare to dishonor His (the Holy Spirit's) great work and not tell you the whole truth. Not just the part you want to hear. Although I must admit this book is not for the faint of heart, that's how the Holy Spirit gives it to me. Thank you for your thirst for the truth. Let's continue, shall we?

There are three parts to the Godhead, better known as the persons of God: God the Father, God the Son and God the Holy Spirit. We are made up of three parts, we have a spirit, we live in a body and we have a soul (mind will and emotions). This book is comprised of three parts, the supernatural, the tithe and the natural. The tithe connects the natural to the supernatural.

In the mid-nineties, a revival came to Brownsville, Florida to Pastor John Kilpatrick's church (correction—God's church). I was attending Bethel Temple in Hampton, Virginia and we too were in the midst of a revival. I had only been saved a few years and this was a brand new experience for me. We had several powerful well-known guest speakers coming and participating in this revival. Night after night I watched the power of God touch people, heal them, deliver them and set them free from alcohol and drug addiction and homosexuality. I remember one night that a lady received her healing from lupus. I know that there is no known cure for lupus but you will have to take that up with God. Our services would continue until one and two o'clock in the morning. There would be people lying in the aisles and under the pews that had been touched by the power of God. I was a catcher and I helped the ushers as the pastors prayed for people night after night. This continued for almost three years.

One night our special guest speaker was an Evangelist from Brownsville and I was assigned to catch for him. After he finished speaking, he began praying for people. The prayer team had also been released to pray for the people and the power of God was just ministering to people all across the sanctuary. I thought to myself, "God, why don't I feel what these people are feeling?" Later that night when he had finished praying for the last person, he turned and thanked me for helping him and then he said, "Now let me pray for you." I would like to tell you that I too felt the power of God but I just stood there like a bump on a log, wondering what was wrong with me. Then he said to me, "You want to feel God's power the way the others do. God said that you have a servant's heart and you will know his power." He turned and walked back to the Pastor's ready-room.

I knew that I had a call on my life to teach biblical principles of finances and I was waiting desperately for God to open a door for me to teach these principles. At that time, I had walked away from a twenty-year profession and I believed God would open doors for me to do what he called me to do. One day I was standing in my kitchen, and as I was washing the dishes, I looked out into our backyard. I saw a very large and tall pine tree that was dying in my backyard. I had been out of work almost two years and no doors had opened for me to teach full-time. Actually, several had been shut. I had many people tell me to go back to my work, even those who were close to me. I looked up at that tree realizing that it was a danger to my family and to our house. It would cost about four or five hundred dollars to have it removed. In my frustration I said, "God, why can't I go back to work and do ministry too?" I found out about a year later, after I had returned to work, that this was not God's best for me.

It was as though God was saying, "That's not what I want for you, but if that is what you want, then ok." Doesn't it remind you of what Israel did when they wanted a King and God said, "I am your King?" They wanted a King like everyone else. Therefore, God told the prophet Samuel to tell them that they could have their King but it wasn't his (God's) best for them.

All God wanted me to do was to open my mouth and speak his word. Speaking words of faith would have provided me with everything I needed to resolve that situation and more. All I needed to do was repeat God's word back to him such as, "And my God shall supply all your need according to His riches in glory by Christ Jesus" (Philippians 4:19, NKJ). "Now to him who is able to do immeasurably more than all we ask or imagine, according to his power that is at work within us" (Ephesians 3:20). "The name of the LORD is a strong tower; the righteous run to it and are safe" (Proverbs 18:10). I am telling you this so that you won't make the same mistake that I did. I listened to the voices of people rather than to the voice of God. I allowed fear of lack to speak louder than my belief in God's provision. As a result, I delayed God's plan for me. Thank God, I am back on track, the Bible says "For all things work together for good for those who love the lord and are called according to his purpose." (Romans 8:28, NIV)

One day I received an invitation in the mail to attend a financial seminar on biblical principles. I was very curious to see what it was all about, the flyer said reserved for pastors and staff. I wasn't a Pastor and I was not on staff at my church at the time. So I said to myself "God how can I attend this seminar if I don't meet the requirements?" Then the thought came to me, "You're a minister of finance and you are a Deacon aren't you?" I had been teaching biblical principles of finance in the adult education program at our church for several years. I wanted to use this seminar as a tool to measure my knowledge on the subject. There weren't many opportunities like this available to me at the time because there were very few ministries that devoted themselves to the subject of God's financial plan. There were only about two days left to register, so I called my wife and asked her to pray about whether or not I should attend this seminar.

I had only been back at work a few months. When I returned to work for the company, I had lost all my vacation and sick leave benefits. Even though I had over twenty years with the company, I had to start over as a rookie. Therefore, I only had about two days vacation remaining for the remainder of that year to cover any sick leave or vacation time. In order for me to attend this conference, I would have to use one of the vacation days and pay the registration fee.

My wife called me back and said that she had prayed and she believed I should go to the seminar. She told me that as she prayed God told her to ask me "How could He invest in me, if I wasn't willing to invest in Him?" We are always looking for God to move in our lives but as soon as God requires something from us (money, time or commitment) we often lose our enthusiasm and pull back. I knew in my heart that what my wife said was God speaking through her. I thought to myself "How can I expect so much from God and not be willing to give up one day's pay?" I asked my wife to call and register me for the seminar and she did.

Two weeks later, I was standing at the registration table at the seminar. I signed in and picked up my name tag. Then I proceeded into a small conference room that held about a hundred people. I sat in the front row because I wanted to make sure I wouldn't miss anything.

The speaker came out, greeted everyone, and began to talk about the Church and taxes. I found it to be very interesting but I was not a Pastor and most of it didn't apply directly to me. However, because I was a Deacon at our church I did find some of the information very valuable. After about forty-five minutes I said to myself, "Well, I guess I blew this one. This is not what I thought it would be at all." Just as I finished my thought the speaker said, "I will be done in about ten minutes and then our main speaker Bishop Meares will be out to talk to you about tithing." I was stunned, I thought that he was the main speaker and that was it. He continued speaking about fifteen minutes more and the first session ended. There was about an hour intermission for lunch and then we returned to the conference room for the second session.

When Bishop Meares came out, I saw this chubby guy with a really nice beard and big smile. He looked like the Pillsbury doughboy with a beard. He began to talk about tithing in a way I had never heard before. I sat there like a sponge in a swimming pool, I absorbed every ounce of knowledge that I could get. I remembered what the Pastor from Brownsville had told me. I could feel the presence and the power of God. Oh no, I didn't fall on the floor or shake or speak in tongues, but I felt like I was in the river of God and it was flowing over me, wave after wave. It was that river that I had heard my Pastor talk about so many times during our revival. Now here I was with the river flowing over me wave after wave. I had forgotten that there were other people in the room with me. It was as though every word was meant just for me. I was like a Lacrosse goalie and I wasn't letting anything get pass me! I was learning so much, it was like finding the final pieces to a huge puzzle.

For years, I wondered why the church was so divided and disobedient when it came to tithes and offerings (money). As I listened to Bishop Meares it was as though the Holy Spirit opened the door and said," Here are the pieces you were looking for." I was like a young child on a hot country summer's day and I had been taken to the beach and told to jump in.

After the teaching was done, he had a question and answer session. I was amazed at the questions that were asked that day. I did not know that so many leaders in the church had so little understanding about tithes and offerings. There were so many questions that the Bishop had to end the session because of time constraints. He said to them, "I would love to stay longer but I can't. However, our teaching program that we are offering today has all the information you have heard today and it will answer all of your questions. I was only able to give you an outline of the program in the short time I had to share." I thought "What? There is more!"

Then another person took over and began to describe what the program contained. When he told us the price for the program, a silence came over the room. Everyone was so excited only a few moments ago with tons of questions, and now there was silence. The facilitator continued to explain what our options were and methods of payment. I thought, "I would love to have that system of teaching but I can't afford it. Besides, these are churches and they can write it off on their taxes, I can't. Maybe I should call my church and see if they would be willing to purchase it. Then I could get it and they could reimburse me when I get back." Isn't it amazing that when it comes to spending money on the things of God, we can come up with excuses, even when we know that it will change our lives for the better.

I remember the Bishop getting up and saying, "Some of you are not doing what God is telling you to do." Then The Holy Spirit reminded me of what God had said to my wife earlier (how could he invest in me if I wasn't willing to invest in him). Now it all made sense. I thought that I was really doing something special when I gave up a day's pay and the cost of the registration to come to this seminar. I even left my wallet in my truck so that I wouldn't buy anything. In the Bible, King David said, "But the king replied to Araunah, "No, I insist on paying you for it. I will not sacrifice to the LORD my God burnt offerings that cost me nothing." So David bought the threshing floor and the oxen and paid fifty shekels of silver for them" (2 Samuel 24:24.) When the Holy Spirit reminded me of this, I got up from the front row as the Bishop was talking and I went out to my truck and got my wallet. When I returned, only a few people were placing orders. I got in the line and purchased the system. I couldn't wait to get home and begin to hear the entire teaching. I was so excited all I could think about was what I had heard. The thought entered my mind, "Do you know how much money you just spent? How do you plan to get it back?" I didn't care I knew what I had found was worth far more than what I paid for it.

I had found the piece of the puzzle that would make my teaching complete. I said, "Thank you Jesus, Thank you! Thank you! Thank you!" Since then God has provided many opportunities for me to share the knowledge he taught me that day. One night I had just finished teaching in Uganda, Africa and the thought came to me, "God I had asked you to allow me to teach your financial plan all over the country and you have taken me to Ireland and now to Africa. God you are taking me all over the world." Our God is an awesome God!

What I am about to share with you about tithing will require you to turn off all of your preconceived beliefs, open up your heart and mind, and allow the Holy Spirit to reveal the truth to you. The way that only the Holy Spirit can! You might say, "Well I don't know this Holy Spirit." Do you really think you could have read this far without His help?

The Tithe and the Covenant, Blessing of God;

In laymen's terms, the tithe is an agreement between God and man. This agreement in the Bible is known as a covenant. Well, what's a covenant? I am glad you asked! A covenant is a term that is foreign to our culture today. We make covenants all the time but just like sin, we have renamed it so we don't have to deal with consequences when we violate the terms. We call sin *our problem* and we call covenants *contracts*, because a contract can be broken, (people do it all the time) but a covenant can't be broken. Like sin, just because we changed the name we think it doesn't mean anything. According to God's word, the price is still the same. "For the wages of sin is death, but the gift of God is eternal life in Christ Jesus our Lord." (Romans 6:23)

The Webster's New Collegiate Dictionary's definitions of covenant are: *(1) an agreement between two or more parties to certain terms, (2) a pledge, a vow or promise (we know it as a contract), (3) In Theology, the covenant of works is that implied in the commands and promise of God to man.* Man's obedience to God entitled him to a happy and abundant life. In the Bible God's word instructed man to obey his commands and live or disobey his commands and die. The Bible says, "If you fully obey the LORD your God and carefully follow all his commands I give you today, the LORD your God will set you high above all the nations on earth. All these blessings will come upon you and accompany you if you obey the LORD your God"(Deut. 28:1-2). On the other side of this, "However, if you do not obey the LORD your God and do not carefully follow all his commands and decrees I am giving you today, all these curses will come upon you and overtake you"(Deuteronomy 28:15). As you can see from the beginning of life, it's all about choices.

It all began with Adam and Eve in the Garden of Eden, when Eve ate the fruit and gave it to Adam. By the way, when Eve ate the fruit nothing changed because she wasn't in charge. It wasn't until Adam neglected his authority and disobeyed God that things changed. God said that they could eat of every tree in the garden except one, the tree of knowledge of good and evil. Then the LORD God took the man and put him in the garden of Eden to tend and keep it. And the LORD God commanded the man, saying, "Of every tree of the garden you may freely eat; but of the tree of the knowledge of good and evil you shall not eat, for in the day that you eat of it you shall surely die." (Gen. 1:15–17 NKJ)

That's how we got into this mess that we are in today. Most people know the story of Adam and Eve—some of us have known this story since childhood. The problem is that to most of us it was just a story. We have no idea of the impact it still has on our lives today. Before this act of disobedience in the garden took place, there was no need for a covenant or an agreement between God and man, because God and man were close. The Bible says "And they heard the voice of the LORD God walking in the garden in the cool of the day: and Adam and his wife hid themselves from the presence of the LORD God amongst the trees of the garden. And the LORD God called unto Adam, and said unto him, Where art thou? And he said, I heard thy voice in the garden, and I was afraid, because I was naked; and I hid myself. And he said, Who told thee that thou wast naked? Hast thou eaten of the tree, whereof I commanded thee that thou shouldest not eat?" (Gen. 3:8–11). As you can see, Adam knew God's footsteps because he was use to walking with God in the Garden of Eden.

When Adam and Eve disobeyed God and ate the forbidden fruit, then God and man were separated for the very first time and sin entered the picture. When sin entered into the world, it was accompanied by death, sickness and disease. Obedience is similar to oxygen in your lungs: as long as there is oxygen in your lungs, you can live a good life but without it death, sickness and disease enters in. When we disobey God's word, we are leaving God out of that area of our lives and whenever we leave God out, death rushes in. This applies to every area of our life.

The Power of Covenant

Since this book is about God's financial plan for your life, you might ask how does this affect your finances? In order to understand the effect on our finances we must first understand the significance of a covenant. When I was a young boy, I loved to watch the old Cowboy and Indian movies on the television. Back in those days, they were called Westerns. I remember if an Indian considered you as a brother, they would perform a ritual and make you what was called a *blood brother*. The two men would take a knife and cut the palm of their right hand and then they would grasp the hand that had been cut and bleeding pressing it into the other person's hand in order to mix their blood together. After this, they would declare themselves blood brothers. This was called a blood covenant.

The blood covenant is the most powerful covenant known to man. It's a covenant that can only be broken by death. In the biblical times, when two people made a blood covenant, they would take and split the backbone of a heifer and lay it open. Then they would walk around the heifer and meet in the middle stating the terms of their covenant (promise). The terms that were spoken went something like this; whatever belongs to me belongs to you, whoever comes against you will have to come against me also, I will protect your family as if they were my own. The major part of the covenant was; **if I violate this covenant (promise), then you could do to me what we have done to this animal!** That is how serious and committed they were to the covenant that they made. What do you think would happen to divorce if we were to hold people *that* accountable to the covenant marriage vows made at the altar?

Our God is a God of Covenant

All of God's promises are based on a covenant. I said earlier that we live in two worlds, a spiritual world and a natural world. We also have two fathers: a spiritual father (Abraham) and a natural father. When we look at what the Bible says, "Now the LORD had said to Abram: "Get out of your country, from your family and from your father's house, to a land that I will show you. I will make you a great nation; I will bless you, and make your name great; and you shall be a blessing. I will bless those who bless you, and I will curse him who curses you; and in you all the families of the earth shall be blessed" (Genesis 1:1-3, NKJ). God does not do anything until he first makes a promise (covenant) to do it. Here God is declaring that all the families of the earth will be blessed through one man. Then the Bible continues to say, "So Abram went up from Egypt to the Negev, with his wife and everything he had, and Lot went with him. Abram had become very wealthy in livestock and in silver and gold. From the Negev, he went from place to place until he came to Bethel, to the place between Bethel and Ai where his tent had been earlier and where he had first built an altar. There Abram called on the name of the LORD. Now Lot, who was moving about with Abram, also had flocks and herds and tents. But the land could not support them while they stayed together, for their possessions were so great that they were not able to stay together. And quarreling arose between Abram's herdsmen and the herdsmen of Lot. The Canaanites and Perizzites were also living in the land at that time. So Abram said to Lot, "Let's not have any quarreling between you and me, or between your herdsmen and mine, for we are brothers. Is not the whole land before you? Let's part company. If you go to the left, I'll go to the right; if you go to the right, I'll go to the left. "Lot looked up and saw that the whole plain of the Jordan was well watered, like the garden of the LORD, like the land of Egypt, toward Zoar. (This was before the LORD destroyed Sodom and Gomorrah.) So Lot chose for himself the whole plain of the Jordan and set out toward the east. The two men parted company: Abram lived in the land of Canaan, while Lot lived among the cities of the plain and pitched his tents near Sodom. Now the men of Sodom were wicked and were sinning greatly against the LORD." (Genesis 13:1-10)

This is a story about Abraham and his nephew Lot. It is very important that we take the time to examine what the Bible says concerning these events, because then and only then will we be able to understand the origin and the importance of the covenant and how it is applicable today. Most people want to be wealthy but they don't want to take the time to learn the principles of becoming wealthy. This is the reason why the lottery and television game shows like the Wheel of Fortune and Deal or No Deal are so popular in our society today. God is not interested in our being blessed one

Most people want to be wealthy but they don't want to take the time to learn the principles of becoming wealthy.

year and broke the next. God's covenant promises are from generation to generation. This is why I am taking this time to lay the biblical foundation for you to build upon. The reason for this is that it doesn't matter what I think, because people can tear my opinion apart. When we base it on God's word then, they will have to get in line with the other people who have been trying to disprove God's word for centuries. Amen! There is an old cliché that says, "If you feed a man a fish you will feed him for a day, but teach him how to fish and feed him for the rest of his life." The Bible says, "Come, follow me," Jesus said, "and I will make you fishers of men." (Matthew 4:19)

The Bible states that Abram had become very wealthy. Abram and Lot's herds had become so large that the place where they were living was becoming too small to contain them. The first thing I want you to notice is that God never told Abram to take Lot with him. Whenever we begin to deviate from God's plan, we are going to run into problems. God is only responsible for His plans for you, not your plans. God told Abram to leave his country, his people (that meant Lot), and his father's household and take his wife Sarah, to a land that He would show him. We also should take notice that in order to receive what God has promised us, we often have to go (mentally) sometimes physically where we have never been before. It takes faith (trusting God) to go against that which you have always depended on even when you know it's not working for you.

When Abram and Lot's herdsmen began to argue, Abram suggested that they separate. Abram told Lot to choose where he wanted to live first and then he would take what was left. Doesn't that sound wonderful, that Abram was so giving? If that is what you are thinking then you need to get over your religious self! I know if I were Abram, I probably would have said, "Lot, I am the one who brought you out here and as a result you have become very prosperous, so much so that we can no longer live together. I am going to move over here and you can move over there. After all I brought you with me." This would have been the response of most people if we were honest with ourselves.

Then the Bible says that Lot looked up and saw that the whole plain of the Jordan was well watered, like the garden of the LORD. In other words, he took what he thought was the best of the land for himself.

Lot, like most people grabbed what looked good and ignored the warning signs around him (how the men of Sodom were wicked and were sinning greatly against the LORD) because that is what he wanted. We often rationalize when we lust after anything (the lust of the flesh, the lust of the eye and the pride of life). When that voice begins to tell us all the reasons we should have it, we often turn off the voice of wisdom and sound judgment (the Holy Spirit).

Abram, however, had a deeper understanding of God's ways (how GOD does things). Abraham understood and valued the power of unity so well that he was willing to give up everything to avoid strife (arguments). What a powerful lesson for us today. The power of unity is one of the most powerful gifts God has given man, but so often we leave this gift sitting on the table of life unwrapped. Why is it that the Devil tries so very hard to keep men from walking in unity? I believe he knows that when we learn to open up this gift and use it, it will be "Turn out the lights, Devil, the party is over." Jesus is on his way!

Let's take a look at what the Bible says about unity: "But the LORD came down to see the city and the tower that the men were building. The LORD said, "If as one people speaking the same language they have begun to do this, then nothing they plan to do will be impossible for them. Come, let us go down and confuse their language so they will not understand each other." (Genesis 11:5-7) This is pertaining to the story about the Tower of Babel. It is a story of the clans of Noah's sons, who decided to build a tower to heaven for their own purpose. God looked down from heaven and did not approve of what they were trying to do. Now we come to the interesting part. Let's examine what the Lord said: "The LORD said, "If as one people speaking the same language they have begun to do this, then nothing they plan to do will be impossible for them." The first thing I notice is that God said that even though they were doing what He did not want them to do, that nothing would be impossible for them. Why? Because they were in unity! I don't know about you but if everyone is speaking the same thing, that represents unity to me.

How awesome would our nation be if we would all seek unity? How awesome our marriages would be if we would seek unity, to really search for a place to understand each other rather than look for each other's faults.

We also fail to realize how powerful and destructive division is in our lives. Why do we have a divorce rate that is going through the roof inside the church as well as outside of the church? Our country is being torn apart at the very fiber because of the decisions of our political leaders. We have ignored what the Bible says about division, "Jesus knew their thoughts and said to them, "Every kingdom divided against itself will be ruined, and every city or household divided against itself will not stand. If Satan drives out Satan, he is divided against himself. How then can his kingdom stand?" (Matthew 12:25-26) The second thing I noticed in this story was the method that God used to stop them from accomplishing what they set out to do (Come, let us go down and confuse their language so they will not understand each other). I don't know of any place else in the Bible that God says come let Us, referring to the Trinity (The Father, The Son and The Holy Spirit) do anything other than create man. The Bible says, "Then God said, "Let us make man in our image, in our likeness, and let them rule over the fish of the sea and the birds of the air, over the livestock, over all the earth, and over all the creatures that move along the ground." (Genesis 1:26) I believe that the power of unity was so strong, that it took the power of the Godhead (the Trinity) to break it. Can you imagine, just for a moment, a life of unity and the power it would provide for your life?

Getting back to Abram and Lot. Now it looked like Abram had given away the farm to Lot in order to stay out of strife and do it God's way. This is what the Bible says, "And the LORD said to Abram, after Lot had separated from him: "Lift your eyes now and look from the place where you are—northward, southward, eastward, and westward; for all the land which you see I give to you and your descendants forever. And I will make your descendants as the dust of the earth; so that if a man could number the dust of the earth, then your descendants also could be numbered. Arise, walk in the land through its length and its width, for I give it to you." (Genesis 13:14-17) When we choose to operate in strife and division, we are choosing to fail. When we choose to operate in unity, we are choosing to succeed God's way. This will not always feel good but God's rewards will always

When we choose to operate in strife and division, we are choosing to fail. When we choose to operate in unity, we are choosing to succeed God's way.

be well worth it. Now who do you think got the best deal? God told Abram that he could have the land as far as his eyes could see. This is a very important principle to your Godly success in life. You will never have that which you don't see yourself possessing. If you can't see yourself having a better job, a better house, a better marriage, a degree or whatever your goal is you will not possess it unless you see yourself obtaining it. It's called faith!

Meanwhile Abram's nephew, Lot, and his family have been captured and are being taken away. "The four kings seized all the goods of Sodom and Gomorrah and all their food; then they went away. They also carried off Abram's nephew Lot and his possessions, since he was living in Sodom. One who had escaped came and reported this to Abram the Hebrew. Now Abram was living near the great trees of Mamre the Amorite, a brother of Eshcol and Aner, all of whom were allied with Abram. When Abram heard that his relative had been taken captive, he called out the 318 trained men born in his household and went in pursuit as far as Dan. During the night Abram divided his men to attack them and he routed them, pursuing them as far as Hobah, north of Damascus. He recovered all the goods and brought back his relative Lot and his possessions, together with the women and the other people." (Genesis 13:11-16) Notice that Abram goes out to battle four Kings with three hundred and eighteen servants that were born and trained in his house. The Bible did not say they were soldiers but servants. Even if they were soldiers, do you think that four Kings, who have just defeated five Kings, might have a few more than three hundred and eighteen soldiers? These soldiers had been battle tested and victorious. Can you imagine one of your relatives asking you and about ten other family members, to go with him to recover his stolen property from a notorious street gang? The street gang you must confront to recover these items are about three hundred strong and they are heavily armed. These were the kind of odds that Abram was facing in order to rescue Lot and his family.

I believe that one of the reasons Abram was successful was because of the unity between Abram and his men. They were born and trained in Abram's house, so there was a very strong bond between them and probably a very strong trust in Abram. After all, I did not read where any of them deserted or fled from the battlefield. The fact that Abram was victorious in rescuing Lot, was to me, a miracle. There comes a time when we must experience the reality of the promises of God for ourselves. It is the foundation necessary for building great faith. It is one thing to read and hear about what God can do. It becomes a totally different world once you experience God's incredible delivering power in your life. Once you have had an encounter with God's awesome power, you become a member of the Blind Man's Club (the man that Jesus healed in the Bible, who once said I was blind but now I see) and then no man on earth or demon in hell can ever take your faith from you.

> **It becomes a totally different world once you experience God's incredible delivering power in your life.**

Abram has an encounter with Melchizedek king of Salem, the Bible says, "After Abram returned from defeating Kedorlaomer and the kings allied with him, the king of Sodom came out to meet him in the Valley of Shaveh (that is, the King's Valley). Then Melchizedek king of Salem brought out bread and wine. He was priest of God Most High, and he blessed Abram, saying, "Blessed be Abram by God Most High, Creator of heaven and earth. And blessed be God Most High, who delivered your enemies into your hand. "Then Abram gave him a tenth of everything. The king of Sodom said to Abram, "Give me the people and keep the goods for yourself." But Abram said to the king of Sodom, "I have raised my hand to the LORD, God Most High, Creator of heaven and earth, and have taken an oath that I will accept nothing belonging to you, not even a thread or the thong of a sandal, so that you will never be able to say, 'I made Abram rich.' I will accept nothing but what my men have eaten and the share that belongs to the men who went with me—to Aner, Eshcol and Mamre. Let them have their share." (Gen. 13:17-24)

When Abram meets Melchizedek King of Salem (King of Peace) and the Priest of the Most High God, he calls Abram blessed by God Most High and he brings out bread and wine. Does bread and wine remind you of anything? How about communion at your church or The Lord's Supper? Then he reminds Abram that it was God who gave him the victory over his enemies. Then Melchizedek blessed Abram and Abram gave Melchizedek a tenth of everything. The tenth here represents the tithe; it is the tenth or ten percent. It represents what belongs to God (I will explain more later). Before, God was telling Abram that he was going to bless him, (future tense) but here Melchizedek blessed Abram, (past tense). Melchizedek was the Priest of the Most High God, the Bible says "This Melchizedek was king of Salem and priest of God Most High. He met Abraham returning from the defeat of the kings and blessed him, and Abraham gave him a tenth of everything. First, his name means "king of righteousness"; then also, "king of Salem" means "king of peace." Without father or mother, without genealogy, without beginning of days or end of life, like the Son of God he remains a priest forever." (Hebrews 7:1-4)

Most scholars say that he was a type of Christ, in the Old Testament Abram gave him the tithe that belonged to the Lord. The King of Sodom told Abram to give him the people that were captured from Sodom and that he could keep the spoils or goods that he captured by defeating the four Kings. Notice what Abram said, "I will accept nothing but what my men have eaten and the share that belongs to the men who went with me. So that you will never be able to say, "I made Abram rich." Abram would not trade the blessings of God for the prosperity of men. How many people have had a promise from God to do something great in their lives and when it didn't look like it was going to happen, they turned away to try something else? Then years later they find themselves lonely, desperate and empty. When we refuse to give up and believe God, the results are far greater than we could have ever dreamed. The Bible says, "Now to Him who is able to do exceedingly abundantly above all that we ask or think, according to the power that works in us." (Ephesians 3:20 NKJ) What would have happened if Abram had not honored God by giving the tithe to Melchizedek? He would have not have been in the position to receive the blessing that God wanted him to have.

> When we refuse to give up and believe God, the results are far greater than we could have ever dreamed.

God begins to make a blood covenant with Abram. The Bible says, "After these things the word of the LORD came to Abram in a vision, saying, "Do not be afraid, Abram. I am your shield, your exceedingly great reward." But Abram said, "Lord GOD, what will you give me, seeing I go childless, and the heir of my house is Eliezer of Damascus?" Then Abram said, "Look, You have given me no offspring; indeed one born in my house is my heir!" And behold, the word of the LORD came to him, saying, "This one shall not be your heir, but one who will come from your own body shall be your heir." Then He brought him outside and said, "Look now toward heaven, and count the stars if you are able to number them." And He said to him, "So shall your descendants be." And he believed in the LORD, and He accounted it to him for righteousness. Then He said to him, "I am the LORD, who brought you out of Ur of the Chaldeans, to give you this land to inherit it." And he said, "Lord GOD, how shall I know that I will inherit it?" So He said to him, "Bring Me a three-year-old heifer, a three-year-old female goat, a three-year-old ram, a turtledove, and a young pigeon." Then he brought all these to Him and cut them in two, down the middle, and placed each piece opposite the other; but he did not cut the birds in two. And when the vultures came down on the carcasses, Abram drove them away. Now when the sun was going down, a deep sleep fell upon Abram; and behold, horror and great darkness fell upon him. Then He said to Abram: "Know certainly that your descendants will be strangers in a land that is not theirs, and will serve them, and they will afflict them four hundred years. And also the nation whom they serve I will judge; afterward they shall come out with great possessions." (Genesis 15:1-14, NKJ)

The scripture says, "After these things." After what things? After Abram brought the tithe to Melchizedek the Priest of the Most High God. Now God is making a blood covenant with Abram. The significance of this is, because it is a blood covenant it can only be broken by death. When is God going to die? Never! So that means that this covenant will last forever. The other important detail here is that God put Abram to sleep and cut the Covenant with himself. The Bible says "For when God made a promise to Abraham, because He could swear by no one greater, He swore by Himself, saying, "Surely blessing I will bless you, and multiplying I will multiply you." (Hebrews 6:13-14) God did this because the lesser cannot bless the greater. What did Abram have to offer God? Nothing! So the lesser Abram could not bless God the greater.

God begins to add to the covenant that he made with Abram. The Bible says, "And I will make My covenant between Me and you, and will multiply you exceedingly." Then Abram fell on his face, and God talked with him, saying: "As for Me, behold, My covenant is with you, and you shall be a father of many nations. No longer shall your name be called Abram, but your name shall be Abraham; for I have made you a father of many nations. I will make you exceedingly fruitful; and I will make nations of you, and kings shall come from you." (Genesis 17:2-6, NKJ) At this point Abraham had no son, he didn't have one son let alone being the father of many nations. He and his wife Sarah had both passed their fruitful years: "Now Abraham and Sarah were old, well advanced in age; and Sarah had passed the age of childbearing." (Genesis 18:11, NKJ)

That's why when you have a promise from God and all the circumstances around you are screaming, "No!" We must stand on God's word (covenant promise) for His word always comes true, it never fails. The Bible says, "So shall My word be that goes forth from My mouth; It shall not return to Me void, But it shall accomplish what I please, And it shall prosper in the thing for which I sent it." (Isaiah 55:11, NKJ)

God also changed his name from Abram to Abraham. Why is this so important? It is unlike the society we live in today where names are often chosen to make a relative happy, because it sounds good, or because you could not think of anything else. In Abraham's day and today in other parts of the world, names have meanings. In America, many Native Americans continue to select names for their children that have specific meanings.

One of the names for God in the Hebrew was Braaa. The people considered God so Holy and awesome that they could not say his name, so they would only say Braaa. God gave Abraham a part of his own name. The Braaa part of Abraham's name, made him a father just as God is our heavenly father. This all started when Melchizedek the Priest of the Most High God blessed Abram and gave him a tenth (tithe) of all. God so honored Abram's faith that He began to add to the covenant that He had made with Abram. The Bible says, "And I will establish My covenant between Me and you and your descendants after you in their generations, for an everlasting covenant, to be God to you and your descendants after you. Also I give to you and your descendants after you the land in which you are a stranger, all the land of Canaan, as an everlasting possession; and I will be their God. "And God said to Abraham: "As for you, you shall keep My covenant, you and your descendants after you throughout their generations" (Genesis 17:7–9). *What is the difference between the promises of God to Abraham in the book of Genesis 17:2–6 and Genesis 17:7–9?* In Genesis 17:2–6, God's promise is directly to Abraham, but in Genesis 17:7–9, it is no longer just between God and Abraham. The covenant has been extended to Abraham's seed (Abraham's descendants throughout their generations). This covenant is a generational promise (covenant). That means that everything that God promised Abraham also belongs to you. This promise from God to Abraham has now become your inheritance. Remember, this is the inheritance sealed in a blood covenant that God made with Himself to Abraham. The only way that this inheritance can become null and void is God would have to cease to exist. It is an inheritance forever.

> Everything that God promised Abraham also belongs to you.

You might say, "How can that be? I am not related to Abraham, what does this have to do with me?" A lot! The Bible says, "There is neither Jew nor Greek, there is neither slave nor free, there is neither male nor female; for you are all one in Christ Jesus. And if you are Christ's, then you are Abraham's seed, and heirs according to the promise" (Galatians 3:28–29). When you accepted Jesus Christ as your Lord and Savior, you were automatically made an heir and added to the inheritance. What was Abraham promised? God said He would make his name great, I will bless them that bless you, I will curse those who curse you, I will have Kings come out of you, and through you all the families of the earth will be blessed.

This is a time to celebrate! Get off your religious horse and start celebrating this awesome news! Most Christians don't know what you have just discovered. Think about how awesome this is! What would you do if an attorney came to your house and said, "Mr. Jones, I represent a distant relative of yours, you do not know this person but he was your great grandfather's youngest brother. He was one of the founders of Bell Telephone Company (now known as AT&T). In his will, there was a provision for the third son of each generation to receive ten million shares of company stock, valued at one hundred and fifty dollars a share, received when the heir turns thirty years of age.

According to our records, you turned thirty years of age today. All I need for you to do is read over these documents and come down to my office tomorrow and sign the release forms." Now would you still be sitting there like a bump on a log or waiting with baited breath for the attorney to leave so you can yell and scream and dance? Chances are you wouldn't wait for him to leave. Isn't it interesting that when a man makes a promise with contracts (that are often broken), we jump for joy? Yet when we have a promise from God who never fails us, we want someone to bring us proof of Noah's Ark. Will you be like Abraham and believe God?

This inheritance from God is greater than any human inheritance because it also contains eternal life through Christ Jesus. (And if you are in Christ, then you are Abraham's seed, and heirs according to the promise). It is for you and your future generations to come. How awesome is that?

Understanding the Process of Tithing:

Many people are excited about the blessings of Abraham but they don't get excited about the process that connected Abraham to the blessing. The process that connected him to the covenant blessing was that Abraham gave; (Then Abram gave him a tenth of everything). This act of obedience activated God's promise in his life. This is why Satan wants us ignorant concerning the word of God and how his covenant works. Satan uses lies like, "All the Preacher wants is your money."

The Spirit of Debt wants to keeps us in debt so that we will not be in a position to connect to the covenant promise. Satan knows he doesn't always have to stop us from doing something: if he can get us out of position, it will be just as effective. God is a God of timing and seasons and when our time comes, we must be prepared to step into that season. God provided manna from heaven but the Israelites had to go and pick it up. God will open the door of opportunity for us but we must walk through it. What if you were waiting for the elevator to go to the next floor, and while you were waiting you heard someone call out your name? You turned, waved at your friend passing by and as you turned back towards the elevator, the door was closing and you were unable to stop it from closing. You had just missed your opportunity to go to the next level. When we listen to Satan's lies and not obey God and act on his word when he tells us to, the results are often the same.

> God is a God of timing and seasons and when our time comes, we must be prepared to step into that season.

What covenant are we under? Is it the Adamic covenant after Adam, the Mosaic covenant after Moses or the Abrahamic covenant after Abraham? What covenant are you under? I am going to ask a few questions that I believe will help you with the answer to this question.

(1) Do you have a High Priest? The Bible says, "Where Jesus, who went before us, has entered on our behalf. He has become a high priest forever, in the order of Melchizedek." (Hebrews 6:20) Jesus has become a high priest for forever. What does your High Priest do for you? Does your High Priest heal you? The Bible says, "How God anointed Jesus of Nazareth with the Holy Spirit and power, and how he went around doing good and healing all who were under the power of the devil, because God was with him." (Acts 10:38) Does your High Priest bless you? The Bible says, "He redeemed us in order that the blessing given to Abraham might come to the Gentiles through Christ Jesus, so that by faith we might receive the promise of the Spirit." (Galatians 3:14)

(2) Who are the Priests? There cannot be a High Priest without a priest. The Bible says, "But you are a chosen generation, a royal priesthood, a holy nation, His own special people, that you may proclaim the praises of Him who called you out of darkness into His marvelous light." (1 Peter 2:9) Moreover, "Strangers shall stand and feed your flocks, And the sons of the foreigner Shall be your plowmen and your vinedressers. But you shall be named the priests of the LORD; They shall call you the servants of our God. You shall eat the riches of the Gentiles, And in their glory you shall boast." (Isaiah 61:5-6) We are the priest, if you have accepted Jesus as your savior, then you are a royal priesthood, a chosen generation.

(3) What order is your High Priest after? How many times have we heard the question, do you want to be like Jesus and the answer is an overwhelming yes. How can we say yes to that question if we don't know what order Jesus was after. The Bible says , "This hope we have as an anchor of the soul, both sure and steadfast, and which enters the Presence behind the veil, where the forerunner has entered for us, even Jesus, having become High Priest forever according to the order of Melchizedek." (Hebrews 6:19-20) Jesus has become High Priest forever, after the order of Melchizedek. What do we know about the order of Melchizedek? That he took a tenth (tithe) of all from Abram and blessed him.

What does the phrase; *be after the order of* mean? Webster's Dictionary definition: To be similar to or like. In other words for you to be after the order of someone, you must do things similar to what that person does. If I say I am after the order of Bill Gates, but I build cars for a living, would I be after the order of Bill Gates? The answer is a resounding, No! I could only be after the order of Bill Gates if I created programs and software for computers, because that is what the order of Bill Gates does!

In the same way, how can Jesus be after the order of Melchizedek, and not take a tithe from you (given to your local church) and bless you, the same way that Melchizedek blessed Abram? Because that's what the order of Melchizedek does! How can Jesus bless you after the order of Melchizedek, when you have not brought the tithe to him? God's word will never fail. The Bible says, "I tell you the truth, this generation will certainly not pass away until all these things have happened. Heaven and earth will pass away, but my words will never pass away." (Luke 21:32-33)

Many people believe that they don't have to bring God the tithe because it was a part of the Old Testament law. They believe that when Jesus shed his precious blood on the cross on Calvary and he rose again on the third day, ushering in the New Testament, then the Old Testament law of tithing was no longer in effect. The Bible says, "Do not think that I came to destroy the law, or the prophets: I did not come to destroy, but to fulfill. For assuredly, I say unto you, Till heaven and earth pass away, one jot or one title will by no means pass from the law, till all is fulfilled." Matthew 5:17-18 (NKJ)

Even if Jesus did do away with the Law, it would have not affected the principle of tithing. Why? Because the principle of tithing was established between Abram and Melchizedek about four hundred years before the Law of Moses was given to Moses by God. The Law of Moses did not create the principle of tithing, but it was incorporated into the law,

As you have read, tithing is as vital to your life today as it was to Abraham. Tithing is not dead! Maybe your finances are dead because you have believed the lie that "tithing is not for today" or "all the Preacher wants is your money." Now that you know the truth, what are you going to do with it?

CHAPTER 9

Is Your Money Holy?

God prepares Israel for the coming of the Messiah. Many people today are also waiting for the coming of the Messiah (Jesus Christ). In today's theology, this is called the "Second Coming." In the Old Testament, God had his prophet Malachi speak to the Israelites, concerning things in their lives that would hinder them from receiving the Messiah when he comes. The very thing that they had been praying for was about to take place and they were out of position to receive the answer to their prayers. Ironically, the thing that was hindering God's people over two thousand years ago, is still affecting them today and it is causing God's people not to be prepared for the second coming of the Messiah (Jesus).

The Bible says, "See, I will send my messenger, who will prepare the way before me. Then suddenly the Lord you are seeking will come to his temple; the messenger of the covenant, whom you desire, will come," says the LORD Almighty. But who can endure the day of his coming? Who can stand when he appears? For he will be like a refiner's fire or a launderer's soap. He will sit as a refiner and purifier of silver; he will purify the Levites and refine them like gold and silver. Then the LORD will have men who will bring offerings in righteousness, and the offerings of Judah and Jerusalem will be acceptable to the LORD, as in days gone by, as in former years. "So I will come near to you for judgment. I will be quick to testify against sorcerers, adulterers and perjurers, against those who defraud laborers of their wages, who oppress the widows and the fatherless, and deprive aliens of justice, but do not fear me," says the LORD Almighty." (Malachi 3:1-5) Don't shut me out now!

Most Christians and even non–Christians know the scripture from the book Malachi, Chapter 3, Verses 8-10. "Will a man rob GOD?" That is all that they know because when they hear it, their minds default to, "The preacher is going to ask me for my money." The sad part about it, is usually they are right. This scripture has become as common place as when your mother would say, "Eat your food. Don't you know that there are people in other parts of the world who are starving?" Many Churches have used these verses to strongly encourage (to put it lightly) people to give to the ministry. The truth is most people who hear it give out of guilt and because they feel guilty, they don't give generously. Most of the time the offering basket is filled with more folded up one dollar bills than you can find folded napkins in McDonalds. That's because we never take the time to read the scriptures in Malachi Chapter 3 before verse 8.

God is preparing his people for the next level. In order to move to the next level in God, it always requires a time of preparation. Many of our prayers are based on petitions. We are asking God for a breakthrough in our marriage, our ministry, our children, our health or our finances. Before God can answer our petition there must be a time of preparation. When we ask God for something, God says, "Yes, but while I am answering that prayer I have some things I need to do in and through you." What God has for us is usually larger than what we are asking for. When we ask God to bless us in any area of our lives, we are asking God to increase us in that area.

God always stretches us to receive what he has for us, because in order to grow we must be stretched. I often use this example when I am teaching a workshop. I want you to take a moment if you have pockets or if you have a purse, make sure that they are closed. Now I want you to try to get something out of your pocket or purse without stretching it. Go ahead - try it! You see, it is almost impossible to get something out without stretching it, in the same way you can't get anything in without stretching it. That's why when God begins to do a new thing in our lives he stretches us, because what he wants to do in us is so much more. The Bible says, "No one sews a patch of unshrunk cloth on an old garment, for the patch will pull

It is almost impossible to get something out without stretching it, in the same way you can't get anything in without stretching it.

away from the garment, making the tear worse. Neither do men pour new wine into old wineskins. If they do, the skins will burst, the wine will run out and the wineskins will be ruined. No, they pour new wine into new wineskins, and both are preserved." (Matthew 9:16-17)

I remember when God told me to move from Virginia to Washington State. I didn't really know where it was, all I knew was that it was on the West Coast and I had no desire to go there. There was something about earthquakes that I had an aversion to.

It all began one day when I was talking to a friend on the phone and he was telling me about a great opportunity he had on this new project. He explained to me all of the incentives that his company was offering to him to relocate from the East Coast to the West Coast to manage this project. It was a great incentive package and I jokingly said, "For that kind of money I would go too." Well you know the old cliché "be careful what you ask for"? Then he said, "That would be great because I can make it happen!" I immediately said, "I was only joking, I am happy where I am." Then I heard the voice of the Holy Spirit say, "Listen to what he has to say."

About one year later, I was headed to the West Coast. My wife and I had flown out several months earlier to check out the area we were going to be living in. As you probably know, the West Coast is more expensive than the East Coast and the area where we were going to live had beautiful mountains and water views. These views also had a price tag associated to reflect their beauty. We were only a few days away from going there on a house-hunting trip. My wife Randi loves the ocean and she loves the mountains. She said to me, "Frank, do you think we can buy a house with a water view and a mountain view?" My first thought was, "Yeah right!" I wanted to say, "No way, get that right out of your head." The Holy Spirit prompted me to keep my negative opinion to myself and I simply said, "We will see."

The second day of house hunting my wife says to me, "God told her "you'll get your house on the hill." In the area where we were looking, it was rather hilly and I said to her (being smart), "They are all on a hill." Then we went to see a house that our friend who offered me the job suggested we should see. When we found the house, it was in a beautiful community next to a lake but the house wasn't what we were looking for. We asked our realtor to drive us around the neighborhood and we saw this beautiful house under construction. We stopped and picked up a flyer on the house and the first thing I noticed was that the house was about fifty thousand dollars above my price range (I know ladies, typical man). So we headed back to our hotel and got something to eat. My wife suggested that we go back and look at that house again; I reminded her that it wasn't close to our price range. Of course, I lost that battle.

When we got there, I asked the carpenter if he minded if we looked around and he said "to go right ahead. " When we walked in, it had everything my wife had wanted in a house. When we walked on to the front porch, there was a beautiful view of the lake with the mountains in the background. It was as if God had taken her list and placed it all in this house. The house was about ninety percent complete. We left the house (or should I say I dragged my wife out of the house) and we stopped two doors down to look at another house under construction but it was even more expensive. As we began to walk back to our car, the Holy Spirit said to me, "Look back." When I did, I saw the house that Randi loved and it was at the top of the hill and I said, "Oh no God, that's not the house!" We drove away, found a quiet place to park, and began discussing the houses we had seen that day. Of course, it was a short discussion. My wife and my sixteen year old son, Jonathan, wanted the house on the hill.

I explained to my wife how important it was that we stay within our budget. I was making a case that a Philadelphia lawyer couldn't break. We had enough money to afford the higher mortgage, with the sale of our home in Virginia and the income from my new job. But I wanted a safety net, just in case something happened. Then my son just spoke up out of the blue and said, "You guys are talking about what's in your wallet but you don't know what God has in his wallet!" Randi and I both were surprised because Jonathan never interrupts us when we are making financial decisions unless we ask for his input. I know God's voice and I knew that he had just used my son to speak to us. I don't know about you but when God speaks to me, I have only one answer: Yes Lord!

You see, God was stretching us, especially me. I had it all planned out but God had something much better. After one year of living in our new home, the house went up in value a hundred thousand dollars! All because we were obedient to God's voice and moved from the East Coast to the West Coast and God is not yet done.

In Malachi chapter 3, God uses the terms "refiners fire or launderers soap" (For he will be like a refiner's fire or a launderer's soap) these terms represent a purification process. The way you purify silver or gold is by applying a lot of heat. This separates the gold or silver from their impurities. That's where we get the term pure gold or pure silver. In the New King James translation, the Launderer soap is called a Fuller's soap.

When I was a young boy, my dad would buy Fullers soap from the general grocery store. When it was time to take a bath, I remember how rough the bar of soap was. It felt like you were bathing with sand paper rather than soap and if it didn't get you clean nothing would.

In many of our worship services, we sing songs requesting the fire of God to fall down on our congregations. We sing songs like, "Will the fire of the Holy Ghost fall on me." Anything in the presence of a Holy God that is not Holy will be consumed. The Bible says, "Therefore, since we are receiving a kingdom that cannot be shaken, let us be thankful, and so worship God acceptably with reverence and awe, for our 'God is a consuming fire." (Hebrews 12:28-29) That is why God always requires a time of preparation, of purification and of setting ourselves apart when he is about to do something in our lives. Bishop T.D. Jakes is well known for his phrase, "*Get ready! Get ready! Get ready!* " He said that the reason he does this is that God told him to "Get ready!" Today he has a very powerful ministry that affects the lives of people all over the world. The same anointing that will bring blessings on your life can destroy you if you are not right with God (consecrated).

God always sends a prophet to prepare his people for what he is about to do. When God was about to bring his son to the earth in human form, through a young virgin named Mary, the Bible says, "In the sixth month, God sent the angel Gabriel to Nazareth, a town in Galilee, to a virgin pledged to be married to a man named Joseph, a descendant of David. The virgin's name was Mary. The angel went to her and said, "Greetings, you who are highly favored! The Lord is with you." Mary was greatly troubled at his words and wondered what kind of greeting this might be. But the angel said to her, "Do not be afraid, Mary, you have found favor with God. You will be with child and give birth to a son, and you are to give him the name Jesus. He will be great and will be called the Son of the Most High. The Lord God will give him the throne of his father David, and he will reign over the house of Jacob forever; his kingdom will never end" (Luke 1:26-33). God used an angel to prepare Mary for what he was about to do in her life.

John the Baptist is another example of how God prepares his people for what he is about to do. The Bible says, "In those days John the Baptist came, preaching in the Desert of Judea and saying, "Repent, for the kingdom of heaven is near." This is he who was spoken of through the prophet Isaiah: "A voice of one calling in the desert, 'Prepare the way for the Lord, make straight paths for him." (Matthew 3:1-3) Then God asked, "But who can endure the day of his coming?" There was something that was blocking them from receiving the very thing (the Messiah) that they had been praying for. What was the main thing that God wanted corrected before the coming of the Messiah? Who will be able to stand? *The Bible says, "I the LORD do not change. So you, O descendants of Jacob, are not destroyed. Ever since the time of your forefathers you have turned away from my decrees and have not kept them. Return to me, and I will return to you," says the LORD Almighty. "But you ask, 'How are we to return?' "Will a man rob God? Yet you rob me. "But you ask, 'How do we rob you?' "In tithes and offerings. You are under a curse—the whole nation of you—because you are robbing me" (Malachi 3:6-9).* Isn't it interesting that out of all the other areas of their lives that God could have selected to deal with, such as their immorality, fornication, idolatry or adultery, God chose their money! I did not choose it, God did. God clearly said that they were robbing him (verse-8, Will a man rob God?). He challenged them about not bringing the tithe or giving offerings, as he had instructed them to do. Would you have chosen money to be the thing that would have prevented the people of God from receiving their Messiah, their Lord and Savior?

The issue is not about money! It is about a spiritual process, the order of things. This is the system that God created to bless his people in every area of their lives: family, marriage, health, finance, etc. This system is also used to finance the Gospel. The Bible says, "But remember the

LORD your God, for it is he who gives you the ability to produce wealth, and so confirms his covenant, which he swore to your forefathers, as it is today." (Deuteronomy 8:18) The ability to get wealth is directly tied to establishing God's covenant in the earth. You might say, what covenant? The same covenant that was given to Abraham. God said, "Which he swore to your forefathers as it is today." That

The ability to get wealth is directly tied to establishing God's covenant in the earth.

means the process has not changed and if we want to receive what God has for us then we must follow the process.

We follow man's process every day to obtain money, paychecks, monetary gain or whatever you want to call it. When you go to the bank and withdraw your money (notice I said your money), is there a process that you must follow? What would happen if you went to your bank to make a withdrawal from your account without your account number, or without picture identification? You would not be able to have your request processed. Why? Because you did not follow the required process. **Isn't it interesting how we will give more attention to the requirements of man than to the commands of God.**

This system is about building our faith and learning how to trust God. We will trust God to heal our body, protect our children or save our marriage but when it comes to our money, now that's a different story. God wants us to trust him with everything. He wants to have an intimate relationship with us. God wants us to be able to come to him and cry Abba-Father, which simply means our supporter, our sustainer, father I love you. Sometimes it means Daddy help- with the steadfast trust (faith) that he will do it.

The bottom line is, if you do not tithe and give offerings unto the Lord then you are a thief, Sir! You are a thief, Madam! The Bible says, "Do you not know that the wicked will not inherit the kingdom of God? Do not be deceived: Neither the sexually immoral nor idolaters nor adulterers nor male prostitutes nor homosexual offenders nor thieves nor the greedy nor drunkards nor slanderers nor swindlers will inherit the kingdom of God." (1 Corinthians 6:9-10) If your money is not consecrated, if it is not set apart unto the Lord, Then it is not Holy! **God has created a financial system of blessing our lives, but we must be willing to obey God and**

follow his plan and his process in order to access our account. The Bible says, "For I know the plans I have for you," declares the LORD, "plans to prosper you and not to harm you, plans to give you hope and a future." (Jeremiah 29:11)

Will A Man Rob God!

Will a man Rob God? This question is a rhetorical question. Many times, we have heard during the offering ceremony the passages from Malachi 3:6-8. They are read to educate the people as to why they should bring the tithes and give offerings. Most people have become so accustomed to hearing these passages that they go into a spiritual default and reach into their pockets for something or they sit with their fists closed in defiance. Many are thinking, "All the preacher wants is my money."

I always wanted to know what does this mean, robbing God. What does it mean in Malachi 3:6-9 (You are under a curse—the whole nation of you—because you are robbing me) to be cursed with a curse? I had no idea what they were talking about and if the truth were told, you don't either. Most people don't give to the work of God, because they don't understand how it works.

Why does the Holy Spirit use the term rob? Why didn't the Holy Spirit use the term steal instead? I believe it is because there is a big difference between the terms rob and steal. When a person steals something, it only results in something missing, like a television, stereo or jewelry. When a robbery occurs, the emotional stress is much more intense because of the possibility of bodily harm. Let's say for example you are coming home from work early one day and you find a thief in your house in the process of robbing your home. Right away, you would begin to go into emotional distress. What should I do? He hasn't seen me yet. Should I yell out and scare him off? Should I try to stop him? What if he has a gun? Should I just step back out, call the police, and hope they get here in time? What should I do? All the while, your heart is beating like a race horse because you don't know if the thief has seen you. Will he shoot you, stab you, or cause you bodily harm?

The police and the court systems place stealing and robbery in different categories. When the court hands down a sentence for burglary or grand larceny, it is not as severe as a sentence for robbery or armed robbery. Robbery always contains the possibility of bodily harm. The police department has different procedures for handling an armed robbery than they have for handling a thief.

To rob in the Hebrew is "Kima": it means to cover, as in a chalice, to restrain from pouring, to put our hand over. In other words, we block or hinder the flow of God's blessing in our lives. God can't pour out his full blessing on us because of our disobedience in bringing Him the tithe and the offering. We are hindering God's nature to bless the lives of His people and the church. The Bible says, "For the LORD your God is bringing you into a good land—a land with streams and pools of water, with springs flowing in the valleys and hills; a land with wheat and barley, vines and fig trees, pomegranates, olive oil and honey; a land where bread will not be scarce and you will lack nothing; a land where the rocks are iron and you can dig copper out of the hills." (Deuteronomy 8:7-9) God loves us and His plan is to bless his people. We must understand that blessings are a by-product of obedience. It is not bless me first then I will obey. God is not a spiritual Santa Clause, trying to win our approval. The Bible says, "The thief's purpose is to steal and kill and destroy. My purpose is to give them a rich and satisfying life." (John 10:10, NLT)

We cause his body harm when we choose not to obey the commands of God's word. You might say, "How can God have a body? God is a Spirit." You are right. God is a spirit but the church is the body of Christ, the Bible says, "If one part suffers, every part suffers with it; if one part is honored, every part rejoices with it. Now you are the body of Christ, and each one of you is a part of it." (1Corinthians 12:26-27) We are the body of Christ corporately. God designed it that way so that we may perform his work on the earth. When we decide not to obey God in bringing the tithe and giving the offering, we not only harm our own life but the life of our church.

When you hit your thumb with a hammer, doesn't your whole body feel it? You begin to jump around in an attempt to soothe the pain. Your arm shakes your hand vigorously and your eyes begin to tear. Your whole body is responding to one part being harmed, is it not? This is what happens to the body of Christ when we rob God. The entire body of Christ feels the effects.

Your thievery, Sir, Your thievery, Madam, not only affects your relationship with God, it also affects your church. You might say, "I don't believe that I am stealing from God." What would happen if your employer came to you and said, "We did not do as well as we had anticipated this month, so we are going to skip one pay period to make up the difference. We will resume the regular pay schedule two weeks from today." What would you say about your employer? Would you say that your employer did what was best for the company? Or would you say that your employer stole two weeks of your salary? In other words, you have just classified your employer as a thief, because they have taken what rightfully belonged to you.

What if I walked into a store, picked up a digital camera, and walked out of the door without paying for it? The store's security person would stop me at the door and detain me until the police arrived. As they interrogated me, I would assure them that I had never stolen anything before. When they process my case through the justice system, I would still be classified as a thief. Even though I had never stolen anything in my life before, I am now a thief.

The Bible says, "A tithe of everything from the land, whether grain from the soil or fruit from the trees, belongs to the LORD; it is holy to the LORD." (Leviticus 27:30) When we say "God knows my heart, I give when I can or I give what I can, but I can't give the whole tithe (10%)," then God says you're robbing me.

We make God look bad!

We make God look bad to the world by using methods and mechanisms to fund the Gospel that are not found in the Bible. We use chicken dinners, raffle tickets, car washes, bake sales, garage sales and a host of other programs to fund the Gospel. We distort God's image to the world. Instead of a God who provides for his people, a God who showers his people with blessings, a God of abundance far beyond our imaginations. We make God look like someone who had a great idea (Salvation) but can't afford to fund it! We make God look like someone who needs a second job to function. "You do my body harm!" All because of our disobedience in bringing tithes and giving offerings. I believe when the church is 100% obedient to God's financial plan the greatest celebration is going to be from the pigs and chickens, because they can stop being sacrificed for our disobedience.

About ten years ago, I was one of the administrative Deacons in our church, where the financial matters were our responsibility. The board had agreed to lay off staff members because the church budget was not able to support the number of people on staff. I will say that it was an honor to work with my fellow Board Members, consisting of Pastors, Elders and Deacons. I was blessed to serve with a group of men who diligently sought God's will for the people that they served. Thank you, Bethel Temple!

This church body was a very giving church. It gave about thirty percent above the national average. However, God requires one hundred percent obedience to his word. I was very sad that the church, the house of God, would have to apply the worlds system in the church and lay people off from their jobs. In order to be good Stewards of what God had provided, these tough decisions had to be made. Why? Because the Body of Christ (the church) had not obeyed God to bring tithes and give offerings. We had chosen instead to modify it to how we felt. **Remember that the Ten Commandments were not the Ten Suggestions and they never will be!**

CHAPTER 10

Cursed with a Curse!

Satan is greatly influencing the pulpit. He is hindering the blessing of God in the body of Christ. The Bible says, "You are under a curse the whole nation of you because you are robbing me." (Malachi 3:9) If you are a child of God and you do not tithe then you are cursed. God did not curse you but your disobedience opened the door for the curse to enter your life.

Let's say you accepted a new job with a great medical package. In this package, it requires you to pay a certain percentage each month to provide medical coverage for you and your family. You decide that the package is not worth the extra money because you and your family are very healthy and it just isn't worth it.

A year later, you became very ill and you have to be hospitalized. Your stay in the hospital costs you your entire savings and leaves you owing several hundred thousand dollars in medical bills. Did the job bring this financial devastation on you? Of course not. It was your decision not to accept the plan and the terms that were offered to you. In the same way, God does not curse you. But your decision not to accept God's plan and terms leaves you uncovered.

When we disobey God, it doesn't matter who our pastor is or how many prayer lines we get into. The servant (your Pastor) is not greater than the master (God). We can go to whomever we choose and ask them to bless our marriage, health, children, finances or business. You're still under a curse! When God says you're cursed, no man on earth or demon in hell is going to change it! The only thing that can reverse the curse is your repentance and obedience to God's word.

The first curse in Malachi 3:9, in Hebrew means: ARA, which means to execrate. It is the opposite of consecrate or to make Holy, it is not set apart for specific use. Even though you have been saved and set apart, your money isn't. Execrate also implies to call evil down upon you, to invoke or invite evil. When we don't tithe, we invoke or invite evil to come into our lives. It is similar to invocation. Invocation at the beginning of a service is when we invite the Holy Spirit to come and join us. We want him to be a focal point of our service. We invite God's presence into the midst of us.

The tithe provides a covering.

Many times in the Old Testament, before Israel went into battle, they gave offerings unto the Lord believing that the Lord would go before them and give them the victory. Isn't that what you still want today for your family? Jesus said, "And teaching them to obey everything I have commanded you. And surely I am with you always, to the very end of the age." (Matthew 28:20)

When God delivered his people from Egypt, he provided his covering to guide and protect them. There was a cloud by day and a pillar of fire by night. The Bible says "By day the LORD went ahead of them in a pillar of cloud to guide them on their way and by night in a pillar of fire to give them light, so that they could travel by day or night" (Exodus 13:21). God provided for them in the wilderness and for forty years their shoes and their clothes did not wear out ("Your garments did not wear out on you, nor did your foot swell these forty years" Deuteronomy 8:4).

When we come together as brothers and sisters in Christ, we are seeking what is known as a corporate anointing. Many years ago, there was a Sears & Roebuck commercial about a super strong car battery that was called the Die Hard Battery. They would leave several cars out in the severe cold overnight. They had all the cars connected to a harness that was connected to the lights of a stadium. They would leave the cars in sub-zero degree weather all night. These temperatures would drain all the power out of the average battery. With the Die Hard Battery, the cars started the next day. There was so much power still left in the batteries that they lit up the entire stadium! That's the kind of power we generate when we come together in love and unity. We shine so bright that the love of Jesus is seen all around: this is called a corporate anointing.

On Sunday mornings, everything that the Pastor does is to produce an atmosphere or environment where the presence of God can dwell and where the power of God can move in your life through an atmosphere of growth, blessing, healing, deliverance and prosperity. In Wyoming in the winter time, it is very hard to grow anything because of the frigid climate. However, if you have a greenhouse, you can grow many things even though the cold is all around you. Why? With a greenhouse, you can create an atmosphere of growth. You can control the climate, as long as the greenhouse's covering is not breached. The harsh outside condition cannot affect what's going on inside. Like the children of Israel, as long as they moved with the cloud (God's presence) all their needs were provided.

When we rob God, we put a crack in the covering. We no longer have total control of our environment, the Bible says, "When you have eaten and are satisfied, praise the LORD your God for the good land he has given you. Be careful that you do not forget the LORD your God, failing to observe his commands, his laws and his decrees that I am giving you this day. Otherwise, when you eat and are satisfied, when you build fine houses and settle down, and when your herds and flocks grow large and your silver and gold increase and all you have is multiplied, then your heart will become proud and you will forget the LORD your God, who brought you out of Egypt, out of the land of slavery." (Deut. 8:10-14)

The second curse in Malachi 3:9, in Hebrew means Myra: which means to disregard or to abhor (detest). This means that God is not involved in your finances. We have not provided an environment where God can act on our behalf. The Bible says, "And I will rebuke the devourer for your sakes, So that he will not destroy the fruit of your ground, Nor shall the vine fail to bear fruit for you in the field," Says the LORD of hosts." (Malachi 3:11, NKJ) God said when you tithe, that he would rebuke the devourer for your sake.

You may ask what is a devourer. The Webster's Dictionary definition is: to eat up greedily, to destroy or consume; and to swallow completely. The devourer impacts our finances in many ways. The most common way is unexpected expenses such as; the car repairs, the washer or dryer stops working, medical bills or your child needing braces. These are things that occur all too often and at the most inconvenient time. When we don't bring the tithe to the Lord, he has no place to get involved in our situation. We are not under God's covering because we haven't obeyed God's word concerning our finances. It's like walking in the rain with a friend who has an umbrella; as long as you stay under the covering of the umbrella, you remain dry. But as soon as you step from under the protection of the umbrella, you are subject to elements. **Without tithing, God is unable to become fully involved in our care!**

Our tithes and offerings remind God of our situation. The Bible says, "At Caesarea there was a man named Cornelius, a centurion in what was known as the Italian Regiment. He and all his family were devout and God-fearing; he gave generously to those in need and prayed to God regularly. One day at about three in the afternoon he had a vision. He distinctly saw an angel of God, who came to him and said, "Cornelius!" Cornelius stared at him in fear. "What is it, Lord?" he asked. The angel answered, "Your prayers and gifts to the poor have come up as a memorial offering before God" (Acts 10:1-4). This scripture is about a man who prayed and he was a giver to poor people. Notice that he is not a Christian. However, he was a devoted God-fearing man, who wanted to do things God's way. What was it that got God's attention concerning Cornelius? The Angel said, "Your prayers and gifts to the poor have come up as a memorial offering before God," and has drawn God's attention. They were as a memorial before God. Why is the word memorial so significant? What is the purpose of a memorial? A memorial is used to remind us usually of an important place or an event. The Battleship, The USS Arizona, reminds us of the attack on Pearl Harbor and the Lincoln Memorial reminds us of President Abraham Lincoln. The prayers and giving of Cornelius were so important to God, that God sent an Angel to let him know that his prayers had been heard. When our giving is mixed with our prayers, it serves as an email to God about our situation. Our giving reminds God. Our giving provides a place for God to act on our behalf.

Our giving reminds God.

Our giving provides a place for God to act on our behalf.

Notice that the Bible says that God will rebuke the devourer, not you. Let's picture ourselves back in high school; I know some of us will have to think harder than others. The school bully threatens to beat you up after school and all day long, you dread the school bell ringing for dismissal. When you walk outside into the schoolyard, your palms are sweating and you are looking around hoping you don't see the bully.

Just as you think you are safe and that he probably forgot, he appears. As he punches his fist into the palm of his hand repeatedly, with fire in his eyes he walks towards you. You want to run but it's too late and now he is within striking distance. Just as he begins to lunge towards you, the entire football team steps between you and the bully. They look the bully in the eye and say to him "In order to get to him you will have to go through us." That's what God says to the devourer when you obey him in tithing.

When we disobey God, in our giving then we put a crack in the covering and the circumstances of life have an opening to enter. The Bible says, *"Submit yourselves, then, to God. Resist the devil, and he will flee from you"* (James 4:7). One of my favorite Pastors would say, "There are two sides to every coin, so let's flip the coin over." Now it would read, if you don't submit to God, the Devil won't flee. If we submit, the Devil flees; if we don't, he won't! You do the math! This is about Your Church Family, Your Brothers and Sisters in Christ. No, this is not your thing. You can't do what you want to do. This is not Burger King - you can't have your way, without affecting others. It's not about obeying your thirst. It is about obeying God.

The media in our society has flooded our minds with advertisements telling us that we should think of self-first. Over the last, several decades we have become more of a *Me* oriented society and it has even infected the church. You hear people say "My Pastor, my church, my blessing, my God." The term "ours" has almost been eliminated from our vocabulary—we even try to take personal ownership of God.

He is our God! The Bible says, "What agreement is there between the temple of God and idols? For we are the temple of the living God. As God has said, "I will live with them and walk among them, and I will be their God, and they will be my people" (1Corinthians 6:16). God calls us his children. This means we are family. We are all connected to each other. What we do has a direct and indirect effect on other people.

The Effects of Breaking the Covenant

Nowhere is that more evident than in the Bible story of Achan, in the book of Joshua. The Bible says "On the seventh day, they got up at daybreak and marched around the city seven times in the same manner, except that on that day they circled the city seven times. The seventh time around, when the priests sounded the trumpet blast, Joshua commanded the people, "Shout! For the LORD has given you the city! The city and all that is in it are to be devoted to the LORD. Only Rahab the prostitute and all who are with her in her house shall be spared, because she hid the spies we sent. But keep away from the devoted things, so that you will not bring about your own destruction by taking any of them. Otherwise you will make the camp of Israel liable to destruction and bring trouble on it. All the silver and gold and the articles of bronze and iron are sacred to the LORD and must go into his treasury." (Joshua 6:15-19)

Most of us know the story of Jericho. It was a city with great-fortified walls. It was the first city conquered by Israel when they crossed the Jordon. God performed a great miracle. Israel followed God's instructions given to Joshua and made the wall fall by shouting on the seventh day. However, they did not follow God's instruction about the tithe. The Devoted Thing (**But keep away from the devoted things, so that you will not bring about your own destruction by taking any of them**), is the tithe. It was the first city; the first part of it belonged to the Lord. The Devoted Thing was devoted to destruction. The animals that were given to the Priest as an offering unto the Lord were devoted to destruction and placed on the altar. Jesus was the first born, the only begotten son of God. He was also called the Lamb of God. He was placed on the cross as payment for our sins. He was considered *The Devoted Thing*. His purpose was to be a sacrifice for our sins and redeem us from the curse of sin and death. Because of Jesus, who now sits at the Father's right hand side in heaven, we have ever-lasting life. Thank you Jesus!

Before the battle of Jericho, God gave direct instructions about how to handle everything. Achan, however, had a different idea of what he wanted to do. The Bible says, *"But the Israelites acted unfaithfully in regard to the devoted things; Achan son of Carmi, the son of Zimri, the son of Zerah, of the tribe of Judah, took some of them. So the LORD's anger burned against Israel,"* (Joshua 7:1) Achan saw something that he wanted and decided that it wouldn't matter if he helped himself to a few items. After all, they will never be missed. Achan totally disregarded God's instruction through Joshua.

Joshua and the people of Israel had just won a great victory over Jericho. It was like your little league baseball team defeating the New York Yankees' in the World Series.

The Bible says,

But the Israelites acted unfaithfully in regard to the devoted things; Achan son of Carmi, the son of Zimri, the son of Zerah, of the tribe of Judah, took some of them. So the LORD's anger burned against Israel. Now Joshua sent men from Jericho to Ai, which is near Beth Aven to the east of Bethel, and told them, "Go up and spy out the region." So the men went up and spied out Ai. When they returned to Joshua, they said, "Not all the people will have to go up against Ai. Send two or three thousand men to take it and do not weary all the people, for only a few men are there. So about three thousand men went up; but they were routed by the men of Ai, who killed about thirty-six of them. They chased the Israelites from the city gate as far as the stone quarries and struck them down on the slopes. At this the hearts of the people melted and became like water. Then Joshua tore his clothes and fell facedown to the ground before the ark of the LORD, remaining there till evening. The elders of Israel did the same, and sprinkled dust on their heads. And Joshua said, "Ah, Sovereign LORD, why did you ever bring this people across the Jordan to deliver us into the hands of the Amorites to destroy us? If only we had been content to stay on the other side of the Jordan! O Lord, what can I say, now that Israel has been routed by its enemies?

The Canaanites and the other people of the country will hear about this and they will surround us and wipe out our name from the earth. What then will you do for your own great name?" The LORD said to Joshua, "Stand up! What are you doing down on your face? Israel has sinned; they have violated my covenant, which I commanded them to keep. They have taken some of the devoted things; they have stolen, they have lied, they have put them with their own possessions. That is why the Israelites cannot stand against their enemies; they turn their backs and run because they have been made liable to destruction. I will not be with you anymore unless you destroy whatever among you is devoted to destruction. Go, consecrate the people. Tell them, 'Consecrate yourselves in preparation for tomorrow; for this is what the LORD, the God of Israel, says: That which is devoted is among you, O Israel.

You cannot stand against your enemies until you remove it. In the morning, present yourselves tribe by tribe. The tribe that the LORD takes shall come forward clan by clan; the clan that the LORD takes shall come forward family by family; and the family that the LORD takes shall come forward man by man. He who is caught with the devoted things shall be destroyed by fire, along with all that belongs to him. He has violated the covenant of the LORD and has done a disgraceful thing in Israel! Early the next morning Joshua had Israel come forward by tribes, and Judah was taken. The clans of Judah came forward, and he took the Zerahites. He had the clan of the Zerahites come forward by families, and Zimri was taken. Joshua had his family come forward man by man, and Achan son of Carmi, the son of Zimri, the son of Zerah, of the tribe of Judah, was taken." (Joshua 7:1–18, NIV)

Joshua was crying out in grief before God, over Israel's defeat and the thirty-six men who lost their lives   in a battle they should have won very easily. God tells Joshua, "Get up. I am not listening until you get the problem corrected." Remember what I said earlier: "God doesn't hear you when you are robbing him." The Bible says,

Then Joshua said to Achan, "My son, give glory to the LORD, the God of Israel, and give him the praise. Tell me what you have done; do not hide it from me. "Achan replied, "It is true! I have sinned against the LORD, the God of Israel. This is what I have done: When I saw in the plunder a beautiful robe from Babylonia, two hundred shekels of silver and a wedge of gold weighing fifty shekels, I coveted them and took them. They are hidden in the ground inside my tent, with the silver underneath. "So Joshua sent messengers, and they ran to the tent, and there it was, hidden in his tent, with the silver underneath. They took the things from the tent, brought them to Joshua and all the Israelites and spread them out before the LORD. Then Joshua, together with all Israel, took Achan son of Zerah, the silver, the robe, the gold wedge, his sons and daughters, his cattle, donkeys and sheep, his tent and all that he had, to the Valley of Achor. Joshua said, "Why have you brought this trouble on us? The LORD will bring trouble on you today." Then all Israel stoned him, and after they had stoned the rest, they burned them. Over Achan they heaped up a large pile of rocks, which remains to this day. Then the LORD turned from his fierce anger. Therefore that place has been called the Valley of Achor ever since. (Joshua 7:19-26)

All this started because Achan took the devoted things and hid them in his tent. Achan caused thirty-six men to lose their lives because he wanted to do what God said not to do. One man's actions caused an entire nation to suffer. Those thirty-six men had mothers, fathers, wives, sons, daughters, sisters, brothers, aunts, uncle etc. They were family. They were all connected and because of one man's actions, many suffered. They were not aware of what he had done. Achan's entire family was destroyed: his wife, his children, and his livestock. Everything that was his was destroyed. He took *The Devoted Things* that were devoted to destruction (belonged to the Lord) and brought destruction on his entire family.

You might say, "Well, I don't think that's fair. That was back then, people don't do that today." As much as we try to convince ourselves that what we do is no one else's business, we are still connected.

On September 11, 2001, the World Trade buildings in New York were destroyed and thousands of people lost their lives. Did not the whole country feel the devastation, the pain, and the suffering? The entire country was filled with rage, fear and uncertainty.

Months after 9/11, when you finally gained enough courage to get on an airplane, did you feel uncomfortable when you saw someone of Arab descent wearing a turban on the plane? Did you automatically assume that they could be one of the terrorists who brought the devastation to our country? Why? Because you connected them to the terrorists just by the way they looked!

What if someone moved next door to you and they had the last name Dahmer? You and a few of the neighbors welcome him into the neighborhood with cakes and cookies. After meeting the new neighbor, you walked away thinking he was a nice guy. Later you found out that he was the brother of

Jeffery Dahmer, the notorious serial killer. Would you still feel the same way about your new neighbor? Would you let your kids go to his house to sell Girl Scout cookies? We both know the probable answer to that question. What changed? It's called (family) relationship. Just because of his brother's reputation, he will always be affected by his brother's actions. His brother has done him harm.

When we obey God in bringing the tithe and giving of the offering, we open Heaven over our home and our church. It's not about getting cars and houses, it is so much more than that. It is about having the power of the living God, operating in every area of our lives. When was the last time you looked into your spouse's eyes and saw that twinkle of love and joy? Would you like to spend more time with your children at the park, the beach or have a backyard cookout? Can you remember the last time you had a day without pain? How about just waking up in the morning knowing that God is with you?

CHAPTER 11

Switching Kingdoms

T he reason I believe that people don't understand tithes and offerings
is because they really don't understand salvation. Many people
accept Jesus Christ as their Lord and Savior and immediately go
into a survival mode. They are trying to survive long enough to be here
when Jesus comes back. Their main goal is to stay out of Hell and cross
that finish line into Heaven. It's almost like that last person who makes
it into the elevator just before the door closes. I once heard a Pastor say,
"A lot of people are going to heaven but they are not enjoying the trip."
God wants you to enjoy the trip. Many churches sing songs that say, "We
have the victory in Jesus." Then why are we living as if we are waiting
for Search and Rescue to find us?

When we invite Jesus into our lives, it opens up a whole new
world. The Bible says, "Giving thanks to the Father, who has qualified
you to share in the inheritance of the saints in the kingdom of light. For
he has rescued us from the dominion of darkness and brought us into
the kingdom of the Son he loves, in whom we have redemption, the
forgiveness of sins." (Colossians 1:12-14) That means you have switched
kingdoms and you have been forgiven of your sins. Now, not only do you
have the greatest gift, eternal life through Jesus but now you also have
the power not to sin. You are no longer in the victim mode where you
couldn't stop doing things that you did not want to do. **You now have the
power through the name of Jesus to say no to sin and yes to God!**

Some people think that when you receive salvation you go into
a spiritual airport terminal and wait for the rapture flight. We look for
an outward change when the real change takes place on the inside. If

you were graying before you were saved, you will be gray the next day too. If you were vertically challenged before, you will still be vertically challenged after. If you had big feet before, you will still have big feet after. What will change is your attitude about these things. You will learn that you are perfectly and wonderfully made in God's sight. The things you don't want to do, you don't have to do anymore. If the Son sets you free, you will be free indeed (John 8:36). You have switched Kingdoms; you are no longer under the dominion of darkness (sin). You have made a choice to be in the kingdom of light (right living with God).

The good news is that you are now saved. The bad news is that your money is not. You were saved by accepting Jesus and believing in his death and resurrection. Your money, however, is still under the old kingdom you use to belong to. That's why many times when people get saved they find it very challenging financially to operate in their new life. You are saved but your money is not! You have been translated from a Kingdom of darkness to the Kingdom of light. The moment you invited Jesus to take over your life, the spiritual transition was made.

Now your old master Satan has become your enemy. He is furious that he no longer has the power over you to destroy your life. Before you accepted Jesus as your King, Satan did not care how much success you obtained (money, car, houses, or degrees) because he knew once you took your final breath, that your soul belonged to him forever. When you accepted the gift of salvation, God disrupted Satan's plans for your destruction. Satan is very angry with you and he wants to do anything he can to destroy you. Now that you belong to The Kingdom of God, he can't destroy you at will because you have been redeemed by the work of the cross (Jesus' shed blood at Calvary). Your sins were paid for in full and you are now free in the Kingdom of light.

Satan now wants to destroy your testimony. He doesn't want you going back to the places you use to hang out telling people about how good your God is. He doesn't want people to see you happy and prospering in your new life. He wants to make sure that your life is miserable and all those who know you will say, "Ever since he became a Christian, his life has been bad. I don't want any part of that." That's why God wants you to live a healthy, joyful and successful life. The Bible says, "The thief does not come except to steal, and to kill, and to destroy. I have come that they may have life, and that they may have it more abundantly." (John 10:10, NKJ)

God not only saves you but he uses you to save others. We are God's advertisement in the earth for those who do not know him. When they see the grace of God (his unmerited favor) on your life and the joy and peace in your family, then they want to know about the God you serve. How does your **We are God's** business prosper when before you were headed **advertisement in the** to bankruptcy? How did you get that promotion **earth for those who** and you are the newest member on the team? **do not know him.** How did your child get a full scholarship with the best college in the country? That's when you turn your face towards heaven and say, "God did it!" The Bible says, "They overcame him by the blood of the Lamb and by the word of their testimony." (Revelation 12:11) That's why Satan attacks your finances. He wants to destroy your testimony.

Your money is not working anymore. It has not been taken to the place of exchange. In the Old Testament, the only way you could be forgiven for your sins was through the shedding of the blood of perfect (without any defects) animals in sacrifice. Almost all of the offerings were made with animals as prescribed in the laws of Moses. When the people had to travel from a distant land to get to the temple, they would buy an animal(s), pigeons or doves at the temple and present them to the Priest as an offering unto the Lord.

This was done because the animal that was presented to the Priest had to be in perfect condition. If they had to walk that animal a hundred miles to get to the temple, it wouldn't be in very good condition, not to mention perfect. The Bible says, "Jesus entered the temple area and drove out all who were buying and selling there. He overturned the tables of the money changers and the benches of those selling doves. "It is written," he said to them, "My house will be called a house of prayer, but you are making it a 'den of robbers." (Matthew 21:12-13) The vendors who where supplying the animals for the offering were cheating the people and giving them animals that were not perfect and weren't acceptable as an offering. It made Jesus so angry because they had reduced worshiping God to illegal business transactions to make money. The offering had to be an animal for which people exchanged money for their purchases. That's why they were called money changers, the place of exchange.

Once the Priest accepted the offering (the animal) then that person had fulfilled the commandment of the Lord. Then they had placed themselves in a position to be blessed by the Lord through their obedience. They have now taken their possessions and positioned themselves to receive God's protection and blessings.

Many Christians and non-Christians believe that money is evil. They base their belief on the scripture when Satan told Jesus that all these Kingdoms now belong to me and I can give them to whomever I choose. "The devil led him up to a high place and showed him in an instant all the kingdoms of the world. And he said to him, "I will give you all their authority and splendor, for it has been given to me, and I can give it to anyone I want to. So if you worship me, it will all be yours" (Luke 4:5-7). They think that Satan owns the money and that is what makes it evil. But the Bible never said that Satan owns the money or the wealth. The Bible says, "The earth is the LORD's, and everything in it, the world, and all who live in it." (Psalm 24:1)

Where do all the things that we consider true wealth come from? Where does gold come from? Where do diamonds come from? Where does silver come from? Where does oil come from? Where do emeralds and precious stones come from? The Earth! The Earth is the Lord's and everything in it. Considering this, then all the wealth must still belong to the Lord.

Another reason that Christians think that money is evil is because of the scripture that is so often misinterpreted: "For the love of money is a root of all kinds of evil. Some people, eager for money, have wandered from the faith and pierced themselves with many griefs." (1Timothy 6:10) Most people leave out the love of money and just say that money is evil. That's why they only want just enough of this evil stuff (money) to meet their basic needs and hold on until Jesus comes. The Lord said, "But remember

> If God established wealth as a vital part of confirming his covenant, then how will you confirm his covenant without it?

the LORD your God, for it is he who gives you the ability to produce wealth, and so confirms his covenant, which he swore to your forefathers, as it is today." (Deuteronomy 8 :18) If God established wealth as a vital part of confirming his covenant, then how will you confirm his covenant without it? News flash! You won't and that's why Satan wants to keep you separated from the wealth. But to whomsoever will, let him have ears to hear what the Spirit of the Lord is saying. **I pray that is you!**

The Order of Things

Satan has never owned the wealth but he does own the kingdoms of this world. Satan got possession of the Kingdom when Adam sinned in the Garden. We often say that Satan took them but that is not a statement of truth. Satan did not have the authority (power) to take anything from Adam because God gave all the authority on Earth to man (Adam) to have dominion in the book of Genesis. The truth is that Adam gave Satan the kingdoms of this world when he disobeyed God (sinned) and ate of the fruit of the tree of good and evil.

Through Adam's disobedience, he lost the kingdoms, the order of things. The kingdoms are represented by your educational system, your health-care system, your financial system, your communication system, and more. They are not real. They are like props on a Hollywood movie set. On a movie set, they create an environment that looks authentic but they are just a replica of the real thing. When that scene has been completed, the director has the props rearranged to support the next scene. That's why your banking system is constantly changing and our educational and medical system is undergoing constant change.

As an example, take our money. It is not real. I know that this might come as a shock to you but it will not change the truth. Take a dollar bill and read what is written on the front of your dollar, "This note is legal tender for all debts, public and private." It has no real value. What gave our money value was the gold reserve that it was tied to. That meant that whatever we owed in paper currency was backed up by the amount of gold we had in our federal reserve. Most of us knew it as Fort Knox. Again, where does gold come from? Where does true wealth come from? The Earth! **Who owns the earth and all that is in it? It is the Lord!** Case closed. Several decades ago we disconnected our currency from our gold reserve and the dollar has been losing value ever since. This action of decreasing value is called inflation. That's why a car today costs as much as the average house cost in the seventies.

Tithing is the place of exchange.

When you switched kingdoms, you also switched banking systems. Your old account doesn't work anymore. Satan has marked your money and he refuses to allow you to succeed in his system because you are now his enemy. Remember 9/11? When the United States froze the accounts of anyone that they considered a threat or had any affiliation with the terrorists? Satan considers you a threat to his kingdom and he should, so he has marked your accounts.

Let's say next month you are taking your wife to Europe for your twenty- fifth year wedding anniversary. The day has finally come and you both are excited as you board the plane. After a long flight, the plane lands in Paris France and you taxi to the gate. When the plane finally stops and the flight attendant opens the door, everyone begins to deplane. Since you have been flying all night, you haven't eaten for several hours. When you enter into the main terminal, the smell of food makes your mouth water. You walk to the restaurant and the waiter sits you at a good table. You place your order and the food comes almost instantly. When you and your wife have finished your meal, you aren't concerned about the price because you know that you have a thousand dollars cash in your pocket. When the waiter brings the check and you take out your money to pay the bill, the waiter says to you, "I am sorry, sir, but your money has no value here." You say to the waiter, "I have given you more than enough to pay this bill and a large tip, what's the problem?" The problem is that you have switched kingdoms. You are now in the European Union and your U.S currency doesn't work here. You did not take it to the place of exchange to have your currency converted, into their Euro currency. Your money is not working.

> Through our obedience, we give God a place to get involved in our finances.

When we obey God by bringing in the tithe, God places a covering over our finances (In a way, he converts it). Through our obedience, we give God a place to get involved in our finances. God puts a camouflage over our money and Satan can no longer mark it. Now when that promotion comes up, Satan can't tell your money from anyone else's and you get the promotion. When your child applies for that scholarship, God covers the application, Satan can't mark it, and your child is awarded a full scholarship. You see, Satan is a created being. His is not in any way equal to God (as some people think). God is almighty and he can move the props whenever he wants to on your behalf.

I remember several years ago, after being out in ministry for almost two years. God was telling me to go back to work. I was at an all night men's prayer meeting when a brother began to share with the guys what God had laid on his heart. He said, "Someone in here, God is telling you to go back to work. You are saying, 'But God, how would it look if I went back to work?' God says, 'Don't worry about how it will look, it is how you will look that you are really concerned about." I tried to act like God was talking to someone else but I knew he was talking to me. It was one of those times when you want to lean over to the person next to you and say, "I think he is talking to you."

Later I approached the brother and let him know that the word he had spoken was for me. It is not always easy to say what God tells you to say; sometimes it takes a lot of courage. That's why it is important to let that person know that they heard God clearly. This helps to build their faith and encourages them the next time God speaks to them.

Two weeks later, I attended a job fair. When I walked into the room, the Holy Spirit told me to go to the first table. It was the recruiting table for Mechanical Engineering. I said to myself, "There is no reason for me to go there, because it requires a four year degree, which I do not have." I continued on to another table for piping and design. I had a lot of piping experience and I thought I would probably be a good designer. Then I interviewed for two other positions that were not a good fit for me.

While I was waiting for my last interview, the Holy Spirit told me to go back to the Engineering table. Once again, I said to myself, "There is no reason for me to go there, because it requires a four year degree." Then the Holy Spirit said, "I want you to face your fears and go to that table!" Then the interviewer called me to the table I had been waiting on and again it wasn't a good fit either. That was my last interview. As I started to walk towards the door, I was coming up to the Engineering table and the Holy Spirit said to me, "Stop here." I stopped and handed the interviewer my resume. He reviewed it and asked me a few questions and then he said, "Well, Frank, we are looking for someone with a nuclear background and I see that most of your experience has been with non-nuclear systems." I said, "That's correct, I have very little nuclear experience but I am experienced with nuclear interfaces." Then he said, "We won't be able to use you but I will take your resume back to our office and maybe someone there can use your experience." I thanked him for his time and I turned to walk towards the door. Just as I turned, the recruiter sitting next to him, who was interviewing someone else asked me my name. When I told him my name, he asked me if I had mentioned certain forms and documents and I said I had.

He then asked me to wait a few minutes because he wanted to talk with me. I was excited but I also felt bad, because I knew the guy he was interviewing also needed a job to support his family. To show you how awesome and complete God is, the guy being interviewed had a nuclear background so we just switched seats at the table. The interviewer never asked me about having a degree. The only thing he really asked me was if I preferred to work in the office or on the waterfront. Of course, I chose the office because I had been on the waterfront for years. Also, I did not want to see my former coworkers. I found out later, that the man that had interviewed me was the Manager of Engineering.

A week later, I got an offer from my old job as a Senior Engineering Analyst. I really did not want to go back but I knew that God had told me to return. I did not want to see all the people that I once told I was going to teach biblical principles of finances all over the country. My ego had taken a serious beating. I thought as long as I stayed off the waterfront, then I would not see most of the people I knew.

During my first day back on the job, all the new hires (including me) were taken to the Engineering office. I thought to myself, "This isn't so bad after all." When we arrived at the receptionist desk, she said, "There will be someone here in a few minutes to take you to your assigned supervisors. Except you Mr. Reed, you will be going down to our office near the waterfront." This was the last thing I wanted to hear. I wanted to stay right where I was. After about a thirty minute wait, a brash young man walked up to me and said, "Are you Reed?" I replied that I was. He said, "I came to take you to our office. Then he began to tell me how I was not properly dressed because I was going on the boat with him to crawl through tanks. My first thought was that this kid has no idea who he is talking to. I was going through tanks when he was in diapers and I did not intend to crawl through them now or ever again. Then I thought I will just turn around, go back to the employment office and tell them, "Thanks, but no thanks, this was a bad idea." Then I got a check in my heart and I said "OK God! I will not be like the children of Israel. I will not grumble and complain. If this is what you want from me then so be it."

When we walked into the office, my new supervisor greeted me. He told me the entire crew was going to be gone for the next several weeks on a ship check and I was to stay at the office with two other guys under another supervisor. He would see me in two weeks. Then he introduced me to the entire crew and they all left.

I was very relieved that I did not have to go on the ship to perform a ship check.

A ship check is what engineers and designers do to verify all the work that is scheduled to be accomplished. They go on the ship and physically walk through each system before they begin to develop drawings to perform the work. I had no desire to go back to the ship to perform a ship check. My days of crawling through piping systems, tanks, cable ways and bilges were behind me. I performed this duty many times in my ship-building career. It was exciting and I loved the challenge. Now that I am older, I will let the younger people enjoy the task. One of the analysts from the other group began to show me the basics of my new job. This was just to keep me busy until my supervisor returned from the ship. As I was sitting there, I thought, "This was not a good idea. When lunchtime comes, I will turn in my badge and go home. Maybe I didn't hear God after all. Maybe it was just me talking because everyone else wanted me to go back to work."

Then I overheard the other supervisor talking to his right hand man. I was told this guy was very sharp and his supervisor depended on him heavily. The supervisor's right hand man wanted to help his friend get into the Engineering department. He said that his friend had graduated from the Apprentice School and had ten years experience. The supervisor told him that he would love to help him but if his friend did not have a degree, he was doubtful if he could do anything to help him. Then I knew that God had placed me there in that job because there I sat without a degree. I was the only Senior Engineering Analyst in the department – and without a degree! **When you obey God, God will move the props!**

For the next several years, I enjoyed my job, working with some really great people and learning new systems. We had a wonderful Bible study in the conference room during our lunch hour. But deep in my heart, I always knew that God was not done with me yet.

Several years ago there was a song out by Yolanda Adams, entitled "Thank You Lord" and the lyrics went like this: "Why do you thank him so much Yolanda? "They said I could not take it but he said I could; they said I wouldn't make it but he said I would, Thank You Lord! Thank You Lord!" To me, the writer of that song knew that God was in charge and that he would change the props.

Make the exchange. God wants to bless you to be a blessing. God has made a covenant with Abraham that all the families of the earth would be blessed through you. "If you be in Christ then you are Abraham's seed and heirs according to the promise" (Galatians 3:29). The Bible says, "No one can serve two masters. Either he will hate the one and love the other, or he will be devoted to the one and despise the other. You cannot serve both God and Money" (Matthew 6:25). The Bible calls money a master, in other words it controls your life. Through the previous chapter, we have read about the many ways that money, (its called mammon in the New King James) controls our lives.

Remember, you are saved but your money is not. We are to honor God with the first portion, the tithe (10%) and God's protection covers the 90% that is left. The Bible says, "Honor the LORD with your wealth, With the first fruits of all your crops; then your barns will be filled to overflowing and your vats will brim over with new wine." (Proverbs 3:9-10) The 90% will do more when it has been consecrated, set apart unto the Lord, then your 100% ever will do without the Lord.

Do not touch the Devoted Thing (the tithe) because it is Holy and it belongs to the Lord, (You Cannot Serve God and Riches) "No one can serve two masters; for either he will hate the one and love the other, or else he will be loyal to the one and despise the other. You cannot serve God and mammon." (Matthew 6:25, NKJ) One day I was in my devotion time and the Holy Spirit said to me, "Money in the natural is like faith in the spiritual. **Without it nothing gets accomplished!"**

Make the exchange and God will move the props for you too. Don't make the exchange and your money remains marked, it is cursed with a curse (remember Achan and the devoted thing). God has given us free will because he loves us. God created us in his image and gave us dominion. God created us to be like him and he sent his son Jesus to show us what he looked like. Two things that we know about Jesus; One, he was full of love and the other is that he was obedient to the Father's will. In order to be like Jesus, we too must obey the Father's will.

The Bible says, "This day I call heaven and earth as witnesses against you that I have set before you life and death, blessings and curses. Now choose life, so that you and your children may live." (Deuteronomy 30:19) This is an open book test. Answer? Choose life!

Part II
From The Supernatural to the Natural

Earlier I told you that as human beings, we live in two dimensions - the natural and the supernatural. In the previous chapters, I have attempted through the anointing of God in my life, to explain the supernatural segment concerning your financial life. I have also tried to give you a better understanding of salvation (life with Christ).

We will now begin to explore what I call the natural side of our human experience. I like to call this Your Part. Or perhaps I should say Your Responsibility. Yes, I used that dreaded word *responsibility*. Some people consider responsibility to be a four–letter word (bad language) but the people who have been trained to accept it know that it is a vital part of their success. I said in the previous chapter that, "God will do His part (the supernatural) but He won't do yours (the natural). That is your responsibility."

I believe that most people want to take responsibility for their own lives but they are often confused about what those responsibilities are. I want to share with you some things that have brought a great deal of simplicity and effectiveness to my life, especially in the area of finances. As we examine the different principles you will see how simple (but not easy) it is to apply these principles to your life. Notice I did not say easy! Easy is one of the most destructive words to success in the human vocabulary. It is like a swarm of termites to a beautiful house: By the time you notice they are there, the damage has already been done. When a student doesn't study because it is easier to hang out with his or her friends, then when it's time to graduate they find out that easy was very costly. A young man gets his own apartment because it is easier than listening to the rules in his parent's home. Then he finds out that his minimum wage salary will not cover his basic cost of living expenses. This is when the reality of independence can be very painful. When people want to purchase a new car because of an easy payment equity loan yet not take the time to create a budget to see if they can afford it. When that foreclosure notice is placed on their home the fear of losing their home becomes almost unbearable. *Easy in many ways is like sin: it is easy to get into but the exit price is always more than advertised.*

However, when we make a decision to make simple proven adjustments in our lives, it can bring very good results and

unexpected rewards. These practical steps will transition confusion into order and turn frustration into peace.

CHAPTER 12

The G.B.R System

W hat is the **G.B.R System?** The **G.B.R System** is a system that uses practical steps for success, consisting of Goal setting, Budgeting and Record–keeping (checkbook). These are basic steps that any business must have in place in order to be successful. You must begin to look at your life as an investment. As a farmer invests seed to sow into the field, he also expects a harvest - a return on his investment. Before the farmer sows the seed, he knows that there is a process of preparation that is required prior to sowing the seed if he wants the best yield (or return) from the seed. Like the farmer, we must go through a process before we can expect the best return from our efforts in life. God has already done his part. Remember the LORD your God, for it is he who gives you the ability to produce wealth, and so confirms his covenant, which he swore to your forefathers, as it is today (Deut. 8:18). Now what are you going to do with the ability that he has given you?

The first segment of the G.B.R System that we want to explore is Goals. What are goals, and how do they affect our lives? The Webster's New Collegiate Dictionary defines goals as the terminal point of a race; the end to which effort is directed; an area or object toward which players in various games attempt to advance a ball or puck through or into which it must go in order to score points; a written or verbal plan to accomplish a task or an idea. Goals are like a compass in life. Well-defined and articulated goals will always let you know in which direction you are headed.

How Do Goals Affect Our Lives?

Goals affect everything we do in life either directly or indirectly. In every stage of life, we set goals for ourselves. Even as toddlers, we use the ability to set goals in our lives. As toddlers, these little bundles of joy are determined to feed themselves. You remember when they take the spoon and fill every opening in their face with food except their mouth and they are so happy that they did it. Some of you only have to remember back to yesterday. How about walking by himself, when the toddler would pull his hand away, take four steps and plop. If you tried to help him, they would protest. The one I like most is when a toddler attempts to dress himself, that's when the arm is in where the head should be and the head is where the arm should be but he did it! It is a basic instinct of human nature to want to achieve a goal.

When we become an adolescent, our goals change: A later curfew, a first date, to drive the car and to get a driver's license. When we become young adults, our goals change again: Deciding which college to attend, which profession or field to specialize in, how to buy our first car or when to get married. When we become adults, our goals revise once more: When to buy our first house, to have the first child, to build a college fund and, of course, securing a retirement plan. When we become parents our goals continue to evolve, moving from self-needs to those of our children: Our children's education, their spiritual maturity, their social life and their career choices.

The reason we are like this is because God our creator set goals for man from the very beginning. God created us in his image, in order to be like God we would have to be able to create life. We call it child–birth. Also, we would have to reign and be in charge. The Bible says, "Then God said, 'Let Us make man in Our image, according to Our likeness; let them have dominion over the fish of the sea, over the birds of the air, and over the cattle, over all the earth and over every creeping thing that creeps on the earth.' So God created man in His own image; in the image of God He created him; male and female He created them." (Genesis 1:26-27)

God wanted a family. The Bible says, *"Then God blessed them, and God said to them, "Be fruitful and multiply; fill the earth and subdue it; have dominion over the fish of the sea, over the birds of the air, and over every living thing that moves on the earth.*" (Genesis 1:28) God said that they will be my people and I will be their God. This has been God's plan from Genesis through Revelation.

The Bible says,

> Then I saw a new heaven and a new earth, for the first heaven and the first earth had passed away, and there was no longer any sea. I saw the Holy City, the new Jerusalem, coming down out of heaven from God, prepared as a bride beautifully dressed for her husband. And I heard a loud voice from the throne saying, "Now the dwelling of God is with men, and he will live with them. They will be his people, and God himself will be with them and be their God. He will wipe every tear from their eyes. There will be no more death or mourning or crying or pain, for the old order of things has passed away. "He who was seated on the throne said, "I am making everything new!" Then he said, "Write this down, for these words are trustworthy and true." He said to me: "It is done. I am the Alpha and the Omega, the Beginning and the End. To him who is thirsty I will give to drink without cost from the spring of the water of life. He who overcomes will inherit all this, and I will be his God and he will be my son. But the cowardly, the unbelieving, the vile, the murderers, the sexually immoral, those who practice magic arts, the idolaters and all liars—their place will be in the fiery lake of burning sulfur. This is the second death." (Revelations 21:1-8)

In the book of Matthew, Jesus set goals for the disciples before he returned to his Father who is in heaven. We know it as the Great Commission. The Bible says, "And Jesus came and spoke to them, saying, "All authority has been given to Me in heaven and on earth. Go therefore and make disciples of all the nations, baptizing them in the name of the Father and of the Son and of the Holy Spirit, teaching them to observe all things that I have commanded you; and lo, I am with you always, even to the end of the age." Amen." (Matthew 28:18-20) Once again, we see God's goal being unveiled, through his only begotten son Jesus.

Goals weren't man's idea, they came from God himself.

As you can see, goals weren't man's idea, they came from God himself. Goals are a very important part of everyday life. We are constantly setting goals but many times, we don't realize we are doing it.

We haven't been taught how to develop or recognize the importance of goals.

The Importance of Goal Setting:

Goals are one of the most important tools needed to transform dreams into reality. As little children, we all dreamed of becoming that special person in life. We wanted to save the world or do something extraordinary that no one else had ever done before. We wanted to be that astronaut, scientist, doctor, musician etc. But because of the pressure of life, we have all but forgotten what it feels like to dream again.

Something begins to rise up on the inside of you. There is a faint voice saying, "I am here! I am still alive! I am not dead!" That is your dream being revived as it feels the power of life flowing through your mind as you think of what could have been. Even now, you want to silence that voice because you're too afraid of being disappointed and hurt again.

That dream inside of you was given to you by God and if God is for you, who can be against you? **Goals are the lifeline that transform, your dreams into reality.** Goals are needed for direction. Goals are like a compass in life - you will always know in which direction you are headed. When you have a goal, you know where you're headed in life. Have you ever heard a person complaining about his job, going on and on about how unfair the company is, and how the pay was pitiful? When he finally took a breath and you asked him, "What would you like to do if you didn't work there?" His reply to your question was, "I don't know!" That's a major reason why he is there: Because *when you don't know where you want to go, you can end up anywhere.*

Have you ever been driving a long distance on a major highway and the signs read north and south? After driving for a long period, you become uncomfortable because you are traveling south and you haven't seen a sign in quite some time. Even though you know that you have not made any turns, you are still not a 100% sure that you're traveling south. Finally, you see a sign that reads Interstate 101 South, and you begin to breathe easier and enjoy the trip again. No one likes to be in a position of not knowing where they are, on the highway or on the highway of life.

With goals, you will always know in which direction you are headed.

Another tool needed for setting goals is a written plan of action. Why is a written plan of action so important? Your written plan of action is your detailed step-by-step process for accomplishing your goal. The Bible says, "Then the LORD replied: 'Write down the revelation and make it plain on tablets so that a herald may run with it" (Hab. 2:2). God has a written plan of action we know it as the Bible. Another title we could give the Bible is God's Instruction Manual, for life.

I remember when VCR's were first available on the market. Everybody wanted to own one, because you could record your favorite television show up to a week in advance even if you weren't home to record it. Everyone was so excited to own one, but most people never really knew how to fully operate their VCR system. They only knew two steps. I called it the power play, because that's all they knew how to do. **Press power and play!** They never took the time to sit down and read the manual to understand all the different options that were available to them on their new VCR, so they settled for the power and play. Today, we have cell phones and like the VCR's, they have many options, but most of us don't know how to access them. Once again, we haven't taken the time to read and understand the instruction manual.

Isn't it amazing, how a teenager can take a cell phone and make it do wonders? When they get their new phone, the first thing they do is begin to study the instruction manual. They realize that once they have learned how to operate their cell phone according to the instructions, a whole new world in communications will open up to them. Don't you sometimes wish that you could turn that cell phone manual into a world history or geography book?

That's how God sees us (as teenagers) when it comes to studying his word. We treat the written word of God a lot like that VCR and cell phone manual. We haven't taken the time to study it, to discover all the great things that are available to us. We operate in survival mode, living on *Just Get by Street*. Rather than living a life of significance and victory on *Abundance Boulevard*.

Why did God give us the written word to be our instruction manual of how to live life his way? God created us. He could have placed his commands in our memory to be released on a time-release system. He could have told us what he wanted us to know on a need to know basis. Why did he have his word placed in the written format? I believe that God was setting an example for us to follow because God placed power in the written word.

It has been documented by scientists that man only uses approximately 10% of his brain's capability. After sin entered the world through Adam's disobedience, man's brain has been functioning on about 10% of its capacity. I believe that this could also be a reason for the written word. Sin could have severely affected our ability and capacity to remember. The Bible says, "I tell you the truth, this generation will certainly not pass away until all these things have happened. Heaven and earth will pass away, but my words will never pass away" (Matthew 24:34–36). When something has been placed in a written format, it greatly increases the possibility of its completion, providing that the instructions will be followed correctly.

Another tool needed for setting goals is a target date. Why is a target date so important? If you don't have a target date or a date for completion, how do you know when to finish? How many times have you said to a friend or an acquaintance, "Let's get together for lunch sometime, we need to get our kids together, we need to have a girl's night out sometime," and you are still waiting for that sometime to come.

Suppose you want to travel on an airline and you walk through the doors at the airport terminal, up to the ticket counter and said to the agent, "I want a ticket." What do you think the response of the agent will be? The first response from the agent should be, "Hi! How can I help you?" The next response should be, "Where do you want to go?" Then, "What date do you want to travel? What time do you want to travel?" That is why a target date is so important. If you need to be on a ten o'clock flight on Tuesday and you show up at eleven 0'clock on Thursday, then you know that you have not accomplished your goal.

Another tool needed for setting goals, if there are monetary costs involved, is a budget. This is one of the main reasons why many goals are not successful. You must know what your expenses will be in order to prepare a successful plan of action to accomplish your goals. We will talk more about this later.

Goals are needed to maintain Balance

Goals are needed to maintain balance in life, to help us keep a proper perspective and find the joy in living. When I think of the character of God the first thing I think of is love because love is the very essence of God. The very next characteristic I think of is balance. God is a God of balance.

Think about it, the sun has never failed to rise in the east and set in the west. The four seasons have never failed winter, spring, summer or fall. The alignment of the planets have never changed nor the position of the sun and the moon, not to mention the billions of stars and other galaxies that we have never explored. God holds the entire universe in perfect balance and yet he has time for you and me. Have you thought about how awesome, God is?

In order to have a successful life there must be balance in your life. Balance in your life is like the tires on your automobile. When the tires on your automobile are out of balance the ride isn't very smooth, as a matter of fact, sometimes the ride can be very rough. When you take your automobile to the tire shop to have the problem corrected, it can be done with a few minor adjustments. Once the balance has been restored then you can once again enjoy the ride.

Life is a lot like the tires on your automobile, when you are out of balance then it can be a rough journey. However when you take the time to make a few minor adjustments, you can once again enjoy this journey called life. The Bible says, "Only be strong and very courageous, that you may observe to do according to all the law which Moses My servant commanded you; do not turn from it to the right hand or to the left, that you may prosper wherever you go." (Joshua 1:7, NKJ) I believe that there are four important loves that we must seek in life, in order to have a balanced life:

(1) *Love of God.* We must put God first in all that we do if we want God's best for our lives. The Bible says, "Therefore whoever hears these sayings of Mine, and does them, I will liken him to a wise man who built

his house on the rock: and the rain descended, the floods came, and the winds blew and beat on that house; and it did not fall, for it was founded on the rock" (Matthew 7:24–25). We must have a firm foundation in life if we are going to stretch out and become all that God wants us to be.

I often think of my travels across the George Washington Bridge, from New Jersey into New York City. As I was crossing over the bridge, I would always be amazed at the tall buildings that seemed to be just sitting on the side of a cliff. I later found out that those buildings were built into solid rock. They had as much as three stories built below the bedrock surface. That is why they could be built so high because their foundation was imbedded into solid rock. If we are planning to go high in life, we also will have to be imbedded into the rock of our salvation, Jesus Christ. To have good success in life we must seek God's plan for our lives. The Bible says, "This Book of the Law shall not depart from your mouth, but you shall meditate in it day and night, that you may observe to do according to all that is written in it. For then you will make your way prosperous, and then you will have good success." (Joshua 1:8)

(2) *Love of Family.* In this day of anything goes, God still has not changed his mind. We live in a society with a divorce rate that is over 60%. We have children that are being abused and abandoned every day. Our young adults are coming out of our school system unable to support themselves not to mention a family. I will stop here. I think you get the picture.

We have thrown away God's goal for the family and it is causing our country to come apart at the seams. The very thing that made America great, the family, is now being devalued and is under a demonic attack. God told us to love our family. The Bible says, "Wives, submit to your husband's as to the Lord. For the husband is the head of the wife as Christ is the head of the church, his body, of which he is the Savior. Now as the church submits to Christ, so also wives should submit to their husbands in everything." (Ephesians 5:22-24) Then God gave the children instructions. The Bible says, "Children, obey your parents in the Lord, for this is right." Honor your father and mother"—which is the first commandment with a promise—"that it may go well with you and that you may enjoy long life on the earth." (Ephesians 6:1-3) God tells us how to deal with developing a family and the order in which the family structure can be successful.

When I use these scriptures, especially "Wives submit to your husbands," I can sense the resentment from women who feel these scriptures are about control rather than God's order for the family. When you get into your car, why do you put your foot on the brake before putting the car in drive? Most people never think about it. It is because the manufacturer recommended it for your safety and the safety of your family. The manufacturer is not trying to control you; however, he is trying to communicate the most effective way to operate your vehicle. God also uses scriptures to communicate the most effective way for the family to operate successfully.

Satan wants you to believe that it is all about your husband controlling you with an iron hand; ruling over you and keeping you in a world of being controlled and dominated. Satan knows that a family that operates in obedience to God's word, with a praying wife or Mom, destroys all of his destructive plans for her family. There has been so much confusion about this scripture "Wives submit to your husbands," for both men and women. Most people never remember the part that says, **"Husband love your wife as Christ loved the church."** How did Christ love the church? He gave his life for the Church.

As my favorite teacher Joyce Meyer would say, "I want to bring balance to what I am saying." I am not telling men to physically die for someone else but I am saying that men need to die to their selfish ways. Turn off the game and go shopping with your wife; buy your wife a new dress rather than a new set of rims for your car. Instead of Boys Night Out for the fourth time this month, take your wife out. **Ouch!** I feel your pain. Dying to self isn't easy but the benefits are well worth it.

I believe that the reason God told women to submit is the same reason nothing happened when Eve ate the fruit in the garden. She wasn't responsible! Adam was! **It wasn't until Adam ate the fruit that hell was unleashed and sin rushed in.** God dealt with Adam, not Eve, because Adam had not protected his family or God's possession (The Garden) that God had given him dominion over. If Adam had taken his rightful place and told Eve, "I can't eat this fruit. God said not to. Let's go over here and pray and I will repent for our family (Adam & Eve)", I believe that Satan would have lost that day.

I always tell people when my wife goes and prays for me, even though I am as wrong as two left shoes. She then remains in right standing with God. Then God says, "Well done my daughter! Now I will go and take care of dumb–dumb (me) and get him back on track." Now! Would you rather have it God's way or the 60% plus divorce rate that we have today? Not to mention the hell you have been living within your house. God wants you to love and protect your family. God wants to bless and prosper your family.

This just came up in my heart, as I was proof-reading this material. I believe that the Holy Spirit spoke to my heart and this is what he said "Many women spend so much attention to the words *submit to their husbands*, that they totally ignore the most important thing that I told them to do for their husbands. I never ask wives to love their husbands. How can you love someone that you don't respect? **The highest form of love that a wife can give her husband is to respect him.** The Bible says "However, each one of you also must love his wife as he loves himself, and the wife must respect her husband." (Eph. 5:13)

(3) *Love of Country.* Some people have said, "All we have in the White House is a bunch of crooks." For several decades there seems to be more corruption on Capitol Hill than ever before. God commanded us to submit to those in charge over us. The Bible says, "Everyone must submit himself to the governing authorities, for there is no authority except that which God has established. The authorities that exist have been established by God. Consequently, he who rebels against the authority is rebelling against what God has instituted, and those who do so will bring judgment on themselves." (Romans 13:1–2)

The Word says that God placed them in that position of government. Notice that it did not say if the person placed in authority was good or bad, it did not say if we liked them or not. The instructions we are clearly given; is to submit to those that have been given authority over you. We also have the responsibility to pray for our leaders. The Bible says, "If my people, who are called by my name, will humble themselves and pray and seek my face and turn from their wicked ways, then will I hear from heaven and will forgive their sin and will heal their land" (2 Chronicles 7:14). According to this scripture, we have a major impact on the state of our country through our prayers. Many of us have spent so much energy on making a living we have forgotten the meaning of life. We pick up a ballot on Election Day, vote for our favorite candidate, and then hope that he or she will represent our needs.

I want to take a moment to talk to young African Americans about the *Love of Country*. I was raised in the south in the 50's. I know about segregation first hand. I was living in Plainfield, New Jersey during the 1968 race riots. I watched the armored cars and tanks roll through our neighborhoods.

About ten years ago, my son Jonathan and I went on a trip to Washington, DC for an all men's prayer on the Mall at the Capitol. There were men there from all over the country, including three bus loads from our church in Hampton, Va. It was an awesome day of prayer and repentance for our country. One of the guest speakers gave us five different categories in which to pray asking God's forgiveness in these categories (repentance). The speaker asked us to get into groups of five and each person was asked to choose a category. Jonathan chose to pray for our country.

The other three men in our group all came from the West Coast. My son Jonathan was eight years old and he wanted to pray for our government. As he began to pray, my heart was filled with pride and sorrow at the same time. I was proud of the passion he had when he was praying for his country. Without a doubt, at eight years old he knew that he loved his country. At the same time, I felt ashamed because I did not have that same passion for my country. My eight-year-old son had to show me what it sounds like when you love your country. One of the men in our group looked over at me and said, "You have a very special boy on your hands." I said I know. I have always taught him God's word and to be honest and loyal with what he believed. The prayers that poured out of him were saturated with love and loyalty to his country. Today he is in college and his love for our country continues to grow.

I, too, have changed a lot since that day. America is my country! My ancestors helped build her with their blood sweat and tears. I refuse to let any devil in hell or men on earth tell me anything else. I don't care what you have faced or what you're facing today: America is your country! God knew that you would come through the trials a champion.

That's why he made you an African American. You are not an African; however, you are of African descent with an African heritage. You are African American and entitled by birth to enjoy the fruit of America. She is not perfect but she is your country. God wants us to love our country and work together to truly make it one nation under God with liberty and justice for all!

(4) *Love of Work.* I know some of you are saying, "Now you have taken it too far." I know how you feel. I use to feel the same way until I found out what the Bible had to say. "Moreover, when God gives any man wealth and possessions, and enables him to enjoy them, to accept his lot and be happy in his work—this is a gift of God. He seldom reflects on the days of his life, because God keeps him occupied with gladness of heart." (Ecclesiastes 5:19-20) I would watch a basketball game and think how great it must be to get paid to do something I would do for free. I thought anybody who can do what he loves doing and create a lifestyle out of it, has to be the luckiest person in the world. When I found this scripture in the Bible, I realized that it wasn't just for a select few but it is available to everyone.

You might not like your job - how does this scripture apply to you? The scripture reads, "Moreover, when God gives any man wealth and possessions, and enables him to enjoy them, to accept his lot and be happy in his work—this is a gift of God." That tells me that God's goal for me is for me to enjoy my work. My problem was that I didn't know God had this goal for me. And because I didn't know, I never asked God what profession I should pursue in life.

Another tool needed for setting goals is faith. Faith is the conductor that is necessary to accomplish your goal. Faith is like a rudder to a ship, keeping the ship on course during the storm. The rudder also keeps the ship from drifting aimlessly when the ocean is calm and it seems like nothing is happening. There are times on your journey to reach your goal that faith will be the only thing that will keep you from giving up. In life as we strive to succeed, many things will challenge us to give into mediocrity. The obstacles may come in many forms: Your family, a friend, society, lack of experience, education or your own self-esteem. The Bible says, "For a great and effective door has opened to me, and there are many adversaries." (1CoR. 16:9, NKJ) Where there is an opportunity, you will find adversaries. Without faith, you will become a member of the *Wish I Woulda, Shoulda, Coulda Club* "spending the rest of your life wondering" what if?

So often the challenges of life causes, many people to give up on their dreams when they were so close to the door of success. The Bible says, "Now faith is the substance of things hoped for, the evidence of things not seen." (Hebrews 11:1, NKJ) When you have faith working inside of you, you can see what other people around you can't see. They see your challenge as a dead end but you see it as a reason to build a bridge to connect you to your goal. Faith is our connection between possibility and reality. The Bible says, "But without faith it is impossible to please Him, for he who comes to God must believe that He is, and that He is a rewarder of those who diligently seek Him." (Hebrews 11:6, NKJ) This is an awesome verse; it tells us of the one thing that pleases God the most. Faith! When we choose to believe God and operate according to his will, then he rewards us for our faithfulness.

Don't get religious on me now! If Bill Gates had just sent you a certified letter saying that he was going to give you a reward for services rendered, your mind would be running around like a kid in a toy store. When the God of the universe says that he rewards those who diligently seek him, (don't lose faith in what he has promised). That's shouting territory!

CHAPTER 13

Three Types of Goals

There are three types of goals that are needed to have a complete picture of what you want to accomplish within a certain time. **The first type of goal is called an immediate goal.** An immediate goal can be accomplished within three to twelve months. When God created man, he had an immediate goal (however, God's plan was not based on this time line). "God blessed them and said to them, "Be fruitful and increase in number; fill the earth and subdue it. Rule over the fish of the sea and the birds of the air and over every living creature that moves on the ground." (Genesis 1:28) God was establishing His image in the earth and man was to be fruitful, multiply and rule. Our immediate goal could be painting the house, buying a new car, losing weight, redecorating or remodeling. These projects can be accomplished in three to twelve months.

The second type of goal is the short-term goal and can be accomplished within two to five years. When God created man, he had a short-term goal (however, God's plan was not based on this time line). "The Spirit of the Sovereign LORD is on me, because the LORD has anointed me to preach good news to the poor. He has sent me to bind up the brokenhearted, to proclaim freedom for the captives and release from darkness for the prisoners, to proclaim the year of the LORD's favor and the day of vengeance of our God, to comfort all who mourn. (Isaiah 61:1–3)

Our short-term goals could be going back to school, starting a family, changing careers, starting a business or buying a house. These projects can be accomplished within two to five years.

The third type of goal is called the long-term goal and can be accomplished within five to ten years. God had a long-term goal for man (however, God's plan was not based on this time line). "And I heard a loud voice from the throne saying, "Now the dwelling of God is with men, and he will live with them. They will be his people, and God himself will be with them and be their God" (Revelation 21:3). As I've said earlier, God had a goal that goes from Genesis to Revelation and that Goal was to have a family. **You!** Our long-term goals could be sending our child to college, buying a summer home, traveling or retiring. We all have goals. Too many times, they are never transformed into reality because we don't have a plan of how to develop our goals.

Developing Your Goals

Establish what your goals are and what categories they belong in: **Immediate, Short term or Long term**. Then apply this process to developing your goals. You will only need to follow seven simple basic steps:

1. Define your goal

    a) To get out of debt

    b) To save $5,000.00

2. Develop a plan of action **(If you fail to plan, you plan to fail).**

    a) Agree to stop spending

    b) Discuss ways to reduce present expenses

    c) Develop ways to increase income

3. Set a target date

    a) June–2010

4. Create a think group of two or more people (that you trust and who want your success), preferably a spouse if you are married.

    a) Have a family meeting

b) Share your plan

c) Discuss areas of concern

d) Ask for ideas

5. Picture your goals in your mind

   a) Hang pictures of your goal where you can see them everyday

   b) If your goals are personal, hang them in a private place like your bedroom

   c) Set a reward for the completion of your goal, such as if we save a $100 this month we can go out for ice cream.

6. Apply Action. Faith without works (action) is dead (James 2:14-17).

   a) Plan your work and work your plan

   b) Be consistent. A quitter never wins and a winner never quits!

7. Keep your faith, for without faith it is impossible to please God

   a) Have family progress meetings

   b) Let each person give a progress report; don't dominate the meeting.

   c) Encourage each other

   d) If one person on your team is struggling, pitch in to help them.

Remember there is no "I" in TEAM

How Corporate America uses Biblical Principles for Success

In the 1980's America adopted a new strategy in performing business. The results were phenomenal with record-breaking profits in the 90's that continued into the New Millennium. Many thought of the process as being revolutionary but in reality, these principles were as old as the Bible. You will see a direct correlation between these strategies and the word of God.

Around the mid-eighties annual leadership meetings by America's major corporations became very popular. In the leadership meetings, they used a seven-step process that was similar to the following:

(1) The meeting would be called to order and one of the top leaders would review progress (or lack of), for the past year.

(2) They would begin to set the goals for the upcoming New Year.

(3) The speaker would present the goal to managers and department heads; They would say, "We will increase sales by ten percent over last year's profit. Although we had a good year, this year will be greater."

(4) The speaker then begins to reveal the plan to accomplish their goals. He would say, "This year we will increase sales by outsourcing five percent of all clerical work. We will add three new automated systems to our production line or we will combine two offices into one and reduce the overhead by twenty percent."

(5) The speaker would request a vote of confidence for these new plans by a show of hands or a verbal yes.

(6) Then the speaker sets the expectation for the leadership by saying, "I believe not only will we meet our goals, but we will exceed our goals." This sets the bar for success and leaves little room for failure.

(7) Then there is an affirmation of faith by closing the meeting with, "Let's go do it!"

This process was used to send the stock market to record earnings and make companies record breaking profits.

These are biblical principles that God has placed in his word for the prosperity of his children. They were given to us (the children of God) as tools to create the wealth that God has given us the ability to get (Deuteronomy 8:18). It's like your child asking you for a new bike for his/her birthday. You go shopping and find just the bike they wanted. You purchase the bike and you can't wait for that day to come when you can give him/her the bike. Now the day has finally come and you give them the bike. Your child's little face lights up with delight, he/she jumps on the bike and rides down the sidewalk showing everyone their new bike. About an hour later, you look outside and your child is playing in the dirt, while all the other kids are riding the bike. How would you feel, watching everyone else enjoying what you have purchased for your child to enjoy while your child is playing in the dirt? How do you think God feels when his children are just getting by while others ride their bike to success!

Three Foundational Biblical Principles for Setting Goals

The first foundational Biblical Principle for setting goals is the spoken word of God. The Bible says, "In the beginning God created the heavens and the earth. Now the earth was formless and empty, darkness was over the surface of the deep, and the Spirit of God was hovering over the waters. And God said, "Let there be light," and there was light." (Genesis 1:1-3) A new idea is first spoken by the person who conceives it. When most people first get an idea to do something, when that light bulb comes on in their mind, they begin to talk to themselves about the process. Let's say you wanted to go on vacation. As you were looking at a magazine, you see a beautiful island that you thought would be a great place for a vacation. The first thing you did was start talking to yourself (self-talk) about how inviting the beaches looked, how blue the sky was, how peaceful and secluded it seemed. Then you started asking yourself, how can I do this? When can I go? How much will it cost? I can't wait to get there!

As you can see, much of the spoken word was an intricate part of the initial conception of your idea. Many times, we don't recognize that we are doing it because it is such a natural part of the process. We begin to speak things into existence, without realizing the creative ability that we are exercising and the power that we are releasing.

We are operating within the same process that God used to create the Heavens and the Earth. The earth was void of light and the Spirit of God was hovering over the earth and God said "Let there be light." *God's words released the creative power and there was light.* Once God gave the verbal command then the Holy Spirit brought it into existence. It is the same process that is used when we speak God's word: the Holy Spirit is released to make it happen.

When you first thought of that vacation, it did not exist for you. You probably thought to yourself "I really would like to go there." Then you said it aloud, "I really would like to go there." Once you released those words, then all of the thoughts began to flood your mind of how you could make it happen. Could it be the same Holy Spirit that brought forth light that's bringing you the thoughts for your vacation?

This is the similar progress that corporate America has used to create the record-breaking gains on Wall Street. They have mastered this process and have applied it to businesses around the world. You will not find many successful businesses that do not incorporate these principles for their success.

The second foundational Biblical Principle for setting goals is the written word of God. "All Scripture is given by inspiration of God, and is profitable for doctrine, for reproof, for correction, for instruction in righteousness, that the man of God may be complete, thoroughly equipped for every good work" (2 Timothy 3:16-17 NKJ). As you can see, the Bible came from the inspiration of God: He wants us to know what his goals are for us. In the corporate world, they realized how effective it was to have goals and a written plan of action. Their written plan of action is a detailed plan, sometimes called the nuts and bolts, of how to accomplish their goals.

Most all successful businesses have what is called a mission statement. I find that to be ironic because companies that don't want prayer or God talked about on their property have a mission statement.

Jesus had given his Apostles a mission statement: "Then Jesus came to them and said, "All authority in heaven and on earth has been given to me. Therefore go and make disciples of all nations, baptizing them in the name of the Father and of the Son and of the Holy Spirit, and teaching them to obey everything I have commanded you. And surely I am with you always, to the very end of the age." (Matthew 28:18-20) This mission statement is known as The Great Commission. Here again someone else is enjoying the bike that God gave his children.

The third foundational Biblical Principle for setting goals is faith. The Bible says, "And without faith it is impossible to please God, because anyone who comes to him must believe that he exists and that he rewards those who earnestly seek him." (Hebrews 11:6) We must believe in God and in his word if we want to be successful in life. The word of God says, "Who satisfies our desires with good things" in Psalms 103:5. It takes faith to go some place you have never been before. If you have never owned your own business then you are a pioneer as far as it is concerned. Maybe you are the first one in your family to go to college - you are a pioneer, too. A pioneer is someone who has to create the path as they go. They don't have the wisdom of other people to guide them through the roundabouts in life. Someone is probably saying what's a roundabout?

Several years ago, our family had the wonderful opportunity to go to Ireland and minister. We were also celebrating our 20th wedding anniversary. When we finished ministering, we decided to take a seven-hour drive down the coastline to the Ring of Kerry. In Ireland, traffic circles are called roundabouts. When you come to an intersection, you must go around this circle until you come to the street that you want to exit onto. This can be interesting to say the least, especially when you are driving on the left hand side of the road and you have two or more lanes to traverse now it gets very exciting! **My wife was doing the driving. That's why I'm still alive to share this experience with you.**

Corporate America has made the process of faith a vital part of their process. People who start their own business or manage a business successfully have already experienced a certain measure of faith to get to where they are in life. These are people who believe they can accomplish goals and achieve dreams. They have had experience in working with others to obtain something that they never had before.

That's why the leadership calls them all together to lay out the plan and give them the vision to help build their faith. They know that once they believe then they will carry that belief back to their departments. There they will start the faith building process all over again. The Bible says, "Finally, brothers, whatever is true, whatever is noble, whatever is right, whatever is pure, whatever is lovely, whatever is admirable—if anything is excellent or praiseworthy—think about such things. Whatever you have learned or received or heard from

Faith in its simplest form is putting action towards what you believe in.

me, or seen in me—put it into practice. And the God of peace will be with you." (Philippians 4:8-9) Faith in its simplest form is putting action towards what you believe in. Many people treat faith as a noun or an adjective, but faith really is a verb because it requires action. **Unless you treat faith as a verb, your goal will not become your reality.**

These foundational Biblical Principles will bring you success in every area of your life: spiritually, emotionally, physically and financially. When you begin to apply, the principles we have talked about (the power of the spoken word, setting goals, developing goals, a written plan of action and the proper application of faith) you will begin to experience new levels of success in your life. The most important thing of all up to this point is this: "But seek first his kingdom and his righteousness, and all these things will be given to you as well." (Matthew 6:33)

CHAPTER 14

The Money Management Plan (MMP)

In today's climate, we live in a fast-paced world. We are a microwave society. We want everything and we want it now! In our pursuit of financial independence, we apply this microwave mentality to our finances. Alas we discover we have almost diminished our finances. It is like aluminum in a microwave oven - there are sparks flying everywhere. Then we run around from job to job or from job to school, hoping that we can regain control before everything explodes.

The reason why so many people live in this state of financial anesthesia is that they feel the pain of struggling from day to day. They do not know how to cure it, so they anesthetize themselves with drugs, alcohol, partying and things they cannot afford. Trying to find some meaning to this ever–elusive drama, they call life when it isn't really living at all.

The Money Management Plan (MMP) or budget is a very powerful tool (or you could say a weapon) for taking back the controls of your financial life. People's minds automatically shut down when they hear the word budget. Their brain goes into default and they begin to think about things they do not like to do such as dieting, exercise and eating healthy. All these things are good for us but most people tend to avoid them. We think what more can I give up? I am already at the end now. Only the people, who have been trained to discipline themselves to the MMP/Budget process, reap the freedom and rewards that it brings.

What is a budget? The Webster's New Collegiate dictionary defines it as: Available or assignable to a particular situation, an account of gains and losses of such quantity, a plan for the coordination of resources and expenditures, the amount of money that is available for, required for or assigned to a particular purpose and to plan or provide for the use in detail. As you can see, a budget has a variety of uses. My definition of a Money Management Plan (MMP) is: **You learning how to manage your money, rather than having your money manage you.**

Several years ago when I was in full time ministry, I was teaching a Sunday school class at our church titled the Spirit of Debt. After teaching for several sessions, the class came to an end. One day Norm, the Superintendent of Adult Education asked me if I had any practical teaching on budgeting and managing a checkbook. He said that he was looking for hands-on things that would help the people manage their finances.

I wanted to teach people about the Spirit of Debt. The superintendent asked me if I would put a lesson plan together within the next several weeks so he could present it to the Elders for approval. I walked away disappointed. We had great success with that class and many people asked me when we were going to have the class again.

When God is trying to take you to the next level, many times he will test your character before you get there. As I sat at home one night in my office, I said, "Ok God, if this is the only door you are opening up for me then I am going to walk through it."

A few weeks passed and I only had two weeks to come up with a lesson plan to be presented to the Elders. I went upstairs into my office and stared at the desk not knowing where to start. With only two weeks left, I knew I was in trouble. I said, "Holy Spirit, You are going to have to do this because there is no way, I can do this in two weeks." Now was that a sign of my spiritual maturity or what? No! But it was a sign of being a spiritual knucklehead. If the Holy Spirit didn't help me, I couldn't have done it even if I had a year to get it done.

As I sat there at my desk, I opened my Bible and the Holy Spirit began to show me scripture after scripture about budgeting in the Bible. I had no idea that the Bible has so much to say concerning this subject. I began to write and the revelations just kept coming. When it came time to turn in the lesson plan, I had completed it with time to spare. God is so awesome!

What the Holy Spirit revealed to me in preparing for that class has forever changed my life. The lives of many people have been blessed tremendously through the understanding and application of these principles.

When the Holy Spirit revealed this revelation to me I was so excited, I couldn't wait to teach on it. I had found a solid foundation for biblical principles in finances that I had never heard taught in the church before. There may have been someone who taught it somewhere else but it was brand new to me. Every time I have heard someone teach about budgeting, it was in a financial seminar type of environment or in a workshop with a quick overview of how to prepare a budget. I had never seen or heard anyone use scripture to substantiate budgeting as a part of God's word.

Over the years I have seen God perform miracles in the lives of people, that were willing to learn and apply the principles of the Money Management Plan (**MMP**).

I remember one Sunday morning I had just completed teaching an adult Sunday school class. The title of the class was *In God We Trust!* I was rushing into the sanctuary because the second service was about to begin. As I reached for the door, a young man grabbed my arm (we will call him Daryl) and he was very excited. Daryl said "Frank I have got to share something with you! I was a little startled, I said "Hi Daryl, what's up?" Then Daryl said "Remember I was in your finance class a few months ago?" I said "yes." Then he said "Well my work schedule changed and I couldn't complete the class. Therefore, I took the work sheet you gave us on how to create a Money Management Plan (MMP) and my wife and I began to use what you taught us. Well I just want to tell you that we are totally debt free! It works! It really works, I hope you don't mind, because I have made copies and have given them to the guys at work." I said of course I don't mind. Praise God!!!

There was so much joy in his face! His eyes were beaming and his smile was as bright as the sun. I was so thankful to God. There is nothing like having God confirm that what you're doing is pleasing to him. Remember, Daryl didn't even finish the course but he took what he had and applied it and God blessed his efforts. **Now that's faith!**

A friend of ours told us about a young lady who went to our church (we will call her Karen) who was having great financial difficulty. She asked me if my wife and I would meet with Karen and try to help her out of her dilemma. We agreed to meet with Karen and try to help her. We called Karen and made an appointment to meet with her at her home.

A few days later, we went to Karen's home and she opened the door rather depressed. We asked Karen to tell us how we could help her. Karen told us how she had recently moved into the area with her husband who was in the military. Karen said that they had been married about a year or more. Then she said that her husband had left her and most of the bills were in her name and she did not have the means to pay them. We prayed with Karen and then I took all of her financial information and we ended the visit. I told Karen that I would create a Money Management Plan (MMP) for her and then I would contact her in a few days when it was completed.

We contacted Karen to setup the appointment, so that we could give her the Money Management Plan (MMP). I was very excited because the Holy Spirit had shown me a way to help Karen to get free from this financial burden. When we went to Karen's house and explained the MMP. Karen seemed to be very relieved. I told Karen that I believed this would really help her. Afterwards we arranged a follow-up accountability meeting. When we went back for the follow-up Karen wasn't there. We were worried and wondered if she was ok? We tried several times to contact Karen with no success. When we saw our friend, we asked her had she seen Karen. She said Karen had moved and didn't know where she was. We were very disappointed because we believed that we could have helped her.

After two years had passed, one day my wife calls me at work and says, "You will never guess who called me this morning?" I asked who? She said, "Do you remember Karen who we were trying to help but she moved. I said, "Yes, she called? Where is she?" Karen says that she is living in Germany, she has remarried and is very happy. Karen says that she and her husband were trying to figure out a plan to pay off all of their bills, when she remembered the budget you had given her. Karen said that she told her husband "I have this budget that this guy Frank Reed, from my old church once gave me." Karen and her husband used the format for the Money Management Plan (MMP) and she says they are now debt free!

Karen said that she told her husband that she had never paid the suggested fee for the MMP. Her husband said to her "You must pay him the fee." Then Karen said, "I will mail it tomorrow and her husband said no, write him a letter and tell him what has happened with our finances." Karen told my wife that's why I am calling you to let you know how you have blessed our life and a letter will be coming in the mail.

I just sat at my desk fighting back tears, realizing how magnificent God is. Even when you think it's not working God is working on your behalf, when you trust him. **(God's ways are not our ways and his thoughts are far above our thoughts!)** There are many other stories that I could add to this but I will stop here. You see, I know that God's Anointing is on this work and God is no respecter of persons, if he did it for them and if you apply it **(MMP)**, he will do it for you.

Even when you think it's not working God is working on your behalf.

Biblical References Supporting the MMP

Let's look at some of the references that are given in God's word. Many of these references you have seen before but I pray that the Holy Spirit will reveal to you the revelation that he gave me. The Bible says, "Moses' father-in-law replied, "What you are doing is not good. You and the people who come to you will only wear yourselves out. The work is too heavy for you; you cannot handle it alone. Listen now to me and I will give you some advice, and may God be with you. You must be the people's representative before God and bring their disputes to him. Teach them the decrees and laws, and show them the way to live and the duties they are to perform. But select capable men from all the people—men who fear God, trustworthy men who hate dishonest gain—and appoint them as officials over thousands, hundreds, fifties and tens. Have them serve as judges for the people at all times, but have them bring every difficult case to you; the simple cases they can decide themselves. That will make your load lighter, because they will share it with you. If you do this and God so commands, you will be able to stand the strain, and all these people will go home satisfied. "Moses listened to his father-in-law and did everything he said. He chose capable men from all Israel and made them leaders of the people, officials over thousands, hundreds, fifties and tens. They served as judges for the people at all times. The difficult cases they brought to Moses, but the simple ones they decided themselves." (Exodus 18:17-26)

When Jethro saw the long hours and the burden Moses was carrying, he told Moses the burden was too much for him. He suggested that Moses reorganize and delegate officials over thousands, hundreds, fifties and tens and Moses would handle only the difficult cases. In other words, budget your work and it will be easier to manage. Now Jethro, the priest of Midian and father-in-law of Moses said, "If you will follow my advice and implement this plan (budget), then this is what the result will be: you will be able to stand the strain, and all these people will go home satisfied." Isn't that what we all want for our families, our business and relationships? **That everyone would go home satisfied.**

The Bible says, "Give, and it will be given to you. A good measure, pressed down, shaken together and running over, will be poured into your lap. For with the measure you use, it will be measured to you" (Luke 6:38). This scripture tells us how we will receive our return on what we give to the Kingdom of God. As you can see, once again, it is a process and not just a hit and miss thing that we do. The process tells us that the same measure we use will determine what our measure will be in return. In other words, if you budget to give a little then your return will be in that proportion. However, if you place in your budget to give a lot then that will be in your proportion.

There is an interesting question in this process: Who is in charge of your rate of return? If you don't know what you are giving, how will you know what should be your return? Would you put your money into a stock program with absolutely no knowledge of the performance of that stock and consider it an intelligent decision? Of course, you wouldn't! At best, you could only call it a risk—not an investment. As an investment, you would have to sit down and decide how much you have to spend and how much stock you could purchase with that amount. Once again, you'd be required to use some form of a budget to make your purchase.

The Bible says,

> "Remember this: Whoever sows sparingly will also reap sparingly, and whoever sows generously will also reap generously. Each man should give what he has decided in his heart to give, not reluctantly or under compulsion, for God loves a cheerful giver. And God is able to make all grace abound to you, so that in all things at all times, having all that you need, you will abound in every good work. As it is written: "He has scattered abroad his gifts to the poor; his righteousness endures forever." Now he who supplies seed to the sower and bread for food will also supply and increase your store of seed and will enlarge the harvest of your righteousness. You will be made rich in every way so that you can be generous on every occasion, and through us your generosity will result in thanksgiving to God. This service that you perform is not only supplying the needs of God's people but is also overflowing in many expressions of thanks to God. Because of the service by which you have proved yourselves, men will praise God for the obedience that accompanies your confession of the gospel of Christ, and for your generosity in sharing with them and with everyone else. And in their prayers for you their hearts will go out to you, because of the surpassing grace God has given you. Thanks be to God for his indescribable gift." (2 Corinthians 9:6–15)

I was only going to discuss verse nine in this section but these scripture changed my life concerning God, the Kingdom and money. I believe once you understand it, it will change your life as well.

Whoever sows sparingly will also reap sparingly and whoever sows generously will also reap generously. Based on what you have just read, who is in charge of how much you give? You are! Now I ask you, based on what you just read, who is in charge of how much you receive? You are! So the next time you begin to complain to God about what you don't have, check your giving. Once again this process requires you to budget, because if you don't know what's going out then how can you measure what's coming in?

Most of us have heard the stories of the Preacher taking all of the people's money. Maybe you might have been one of those people. Many people carry their Bible around to look spiritual or leave it on the coffee table as an ornament until Sunday morning. 2 Corinthians 9:7 says, "Each man should give what he has decided in his heart to give, not reluctantly or under compulsion, for God loves a cheerful giver." It tells us that each person should give what they have decided in their own hearts, not reluctantly or under compulsion. That means that we should have prayed and asked the Holy Spirit how much our offering should be, before we ever get to church.

As followers of Christ, we his disciples should discipline ourselves to stop being bucket-plunkers. When the usher is coming down the aisle, we are scrambling to get to our wallets or purses, so we can plunk something in the bucket. We should have already decided through prayer how much to give as an offering, we should have prayed over the offering and been ready to give it when the offering is taken.

This doesn't mean that the Holy Spirit can't speak to you and tell you to give during a special offering. However, that is the exception not the rule. I am referring to the people who are emotionally moved by a television evangelist or a guest speaker at your church and have not asked the Holy Spirit for wisdom in their giving. Even though it might have been a good thing to support feeding hungry people in another country, how does it honor God when that money belongs to your landlord or mortgage company?

It has been my experience with God that he almost never asks me for something he hasn't already given me. I might have other plans for it like a vacation, a new suit, a weekend with the boys but God has already provided for it. There are times when God will tell you to pledge by faith (as I mentioned in an earlier chapter). However, you don't have to give it until he gives it to you. Just remember in this case, the blessing (return) doesn't come with getting it. The blessing comes with giving it! Another principle that I believe confuses many people, is where it says, "God loves a cheerful giver." I want you to know when I first started learning how to tithe; I didn't have enough left to call it an offering. It was only a dollar and on a good week five dollars and that was rare. I was not happy in the beginning process. I was doing all I could to believe God that this thing would work!

Then I began seeing how God was faithful to his word. He began to give me favor, I would get good deals. Once I needed my house painted and the painter told me that he would do it for seventy- eight hundred dollars. I had a budget that I could not exceed. I told them don't call me I will call you. One of my co–workers over heard me telling someone about my ordeal and he said, "I will do it for you a lot cheaper than that." So that evening he came out to look at the house. I knew the cheapest rate was about twenty-five hundred but I didn't have that either. When my co-worker finished estimating the job, he said, "I will do it for two hundred dollars and you buy the paint." I was so happy I wanted to jump for joy.

It was those types of experiences that helped me grow into becoming a cheerful giver. I began to see God's word come true firsthand because I trusted his word. The one thing that sealed the deal for me was when I had grown in the things of God to not only give to the Kingdom but also give to other people.

God told me to give a member of our church family $500. I had never given such a large amount before, so I asked my wife what she thought about it (if God tells you something, he will always confirm it - especially if you're married). Then about two days later as we were on our way to a Wednesday night service, God told me to go get the money before I arrived at the church, get it in hundred dollar bills, put it in an envelope and write on it, "God loves you." I followed His instruction to the tee. When I saw the person in church I pulled him aside, gave him the envelope and I went back to my seat. After the service, the brother and his wife (who were very dear to us) came up to thank us for the gift but we were the ones who received the greatest gift.

He told us that the night before; he was lying on his face crying out to God that they needed a financial miracle and God told him, "It has already been taken care of!" Do you know what it feels like to have God confirm that you have heard him clearly? Especially when you are learning to hear his voice? Since that day, I have been a cheerful giver. What I received was far more than what I gave (it is better to give than to receive).

The scripture says, "Now he who supplies seed to the sower," and bread for food will also supply and increase your store of seed and will enlarge the harvest of your righteousness. The key here is seed to the sower. Then the key becomes a question: Are you a sower? If you are not a sower, you don't need a supply of seed to sow if you are going to leave it in the barn or, in this case, your bank account. That's why it is important to understand that God looks for people he can give seed (money and position) to so they will use it for his purpose. When you seed into good ground (God's purpose), you always get a harvest in return.

The next part of the scripture says, "You will be made rich in every way so that you can be generous on every occasion, and through us your generosity will result in thanksgiving to God." The reason for your harvest is to make you rich in every way, (since we are talking about finances, I will deal with money). The reason for making you rich is so that you will be generous on all occasions.

I know this sounds great but let's not treat God as if he is stupid! If God has to fight with you for six weeks to get you to give $100 to missions, do you really think he's going to release $100,000 to you without testing your faith?

I remember when I gave my second $10,000 gift to the Kingdom. Do you know that it was easier than my first? How could a person who struggled to give five dollars now give ten thousand with joy? Because God has increased my storehouse of seed. In laymen's terms, God has prospered us. The money I used to pay off credit card debt and consumer debt can now be used to bless others and invest in the Kingdom of God.

The bottom line is this: "This service that you perform is not only supplying the needs of God's people but is also overflowing in many expressions of thanks to God." What would happen if that single mom with three kids down the street was out of food and you showed up with enough food to last for a month? What would happen if the elderly couple you know was without a car and you bought them a new car so they could have dependable transportation? What would happen if that brother in-law that always made fun of you being a Christian was about to lose his house? He had been a victim of a layoff and couldn't find a job and you paid his mortgage for a year? These people know that you are a Christian. Do you think that they might just lift their face towards heaven and thank

God for what you have done? **This is the real Church of Jesus Christ in action!**

This is why God set this system up - to bless you, he wants you to be a blessing. To lend to many nations and borrow from none, to be his hands, arms, eyes and ears in the earth. God wants people to see his love for them through you. The only way we can be what God created us to be is to learn and obey his plan.

Notice I did not mention the Tithe. The tithe is not your decision to make. How much it should be, God has already made that decision for us. The tithe is ten percent of your gross income. I know that sometimes your gross is gross, but if you obey God that will change. **However without an MMP (budget) it may get worse!** Don't keep the tithe - it is the Lord's, it is Holy!

The Bible says, "Suppose one of you wants to build a tower. Will he not first sit down and estimate the cost to see if he has enough money to complete it? For if, he lays the foundation and is not able to finish it, everyone who sees it will ridicule him, saying, 'This fellow began to build and was not able to finish.' Or suppose a king is about to go to war against another king. Will he not first sit down and consider whether he is able with ten thousand men to oppose the one coming against him with twenty thousand?" (Luke 14-28-31) The scripture tells us to count the cost. How many people today would not be in the financial nightmare they are in if they had read and obeyed this scripture. If you had read and obeyed this scripture what condition would your finances, marriage, family, business or life in general, be in today? This process could not be accomplished without a money management Plan (MMP). Throughout the Old Testament, we find written records of genealogies and how much was given for offering. The building of the Temple by Solomon is a good example of how every item was chronicled. They had detailed plans that were given to them by God but they had to place them in a blueprint format. If we are to do anything great or small in our lives, successfully, we will also have to count the cost before we start.

I think one of the most intriguing scriptures about budgeting in the Bible is, when Jesus fed the five thousand with two fish and five loaves of bread. These belonged to a little boy who offered (offering) them to Jesus as his contribution to help feed the multitudes. The Bible says, "Late in the afternoon the Twelve came to him and said, "Send the crowd away so they can go to the surrounding villages and countryside and find food and lodging, because we are in a remote place here." He replied, "You give them something to eat." They answered, "We have only five loaves of bread and two fish—unless we go and buy food for all this crowd." (About five thousand men were there.) But he said to his disciples, "Have them sit down in groups of about fifty each." The disciples did so, and everybody sat down. Taking the five loaves and the two fish and looking up to heaven, he gave thanks and broke them. Then he gave them to the disciples to set before the people. They all ate and were satisfied, and the disciples picked up twelve basketfuls of broken pieces that were left over." (Luke 9:12-17) Jesus and the disciples had five thousand unexpected guests to feed. Actually, there could have been as many as fifteen to twenty thousand people in attendance because they did not count the women and children.

I have asked many people over the years, how did Jesus know that there were five thousand men there that day? These are some of the responses I received; He was the son of God, he knew supernaturally! He guessed and most people said they didn't know. Less than 10% could give me the answer that was in the Bible, "But Jesus said to his disciples, "Have them sit down in groups of about fifty each." The disciples did so, and everybody sat down. **They counted them!** If you have one hundred groups of fifty, is that not five thousand?

We treat our finances the same way we treat this scripture. Rather than find out how they came up with that number. We would rather say I think I have enough in my checking account to cover this check or I think I am almost at my limit on this credit card but I will try it anyway. We go to the Pastor and say, "Pray for a financial breakthrough for me" and if the Pastor said, "The Lord told me to write a check for whatever you need. Brother or Sister, how much do you need me to write this check for?" Could you tell him or would you say, "I think I need."

Notice that Jesus, the Son of the living God who healed the sick, opened blinded eyes, made crooked limbs straight and raised the dead had them counted. Jesus knew exactly what he needed before he ever began to pray and these were the results. They all ate and were satisfied, and the disciples picked up twelve basketfuls of broken pieces that were left over." **There was more than enough!**

In our home when my son was younger, every Saturday when I was home, I would fix pancakes for breakfast. Don't get hungry on me and stop reading now. I learned from my sister, who is like my Mom how to cook them a certain way. When I moved into my own place, she would cook pancakes for me whenever I came to New Jersey. Even today, my sister still cooks pancakes for me when I visit.

One day I was cooking pancakes for my son and I was pouring the oil into the pan. I had noticed several times before how much oil it was using to cook the pancakes. Then I heard a voice say to me, "Why don't you pour the oil into a cup and then dip it out with a spoon into the pan. That way you can measure how much oil you are using for each stack of pancakes that you cook." I followed the instructions that were given to me.

I noticed that when I had finished cooking all of the pancakes, I still had a half of a cup of oil left. Usually I would use much more than a cup to cook the same amount of pancakes. Then I heard that voice again say to me, "When you measure your money the way that you measured this oil, you will always have more than enough left over." I now know that voice to be that of the Holy Spirit. The Money Management Plan (MMP) is a tool that allows you to measure where you are financially so that you too, can have more than enough left over.

In this scripture there is also a hidden principle about tithing that I had not seen after many years of teaching. I often wondered why Jesus only counted the men, when *everyone* needed food to eat. What if one man had a family of four and another man had a family of twenty-four, which was not uncommon in those days? How could you distribute the food equally? I have the kind of mind that likes to know how the process works with anything that I am involved in. I believe that once I can understand the process then I can make the system work - if not make it better.

The thought came to me that the reason they only counted the men was because of the covenant blessing. The Bible says, "It is like the precious oil upon the head, running down on the beard, the beard of Aaron, Running down on the edge of his garments." (Psalm 133:2) The covenant blessing that has been released on the man flows like the anointing oil that was poured on Aaron's head. It ran from his head down to his beard and onto his garments. The blessing flows from a man and onto anything that is under his covering. That is why it did not matter if a man had four children or twenty-four children. As long as they were under his covering they would be provided for.

This is the same principle as tithing. Once we consecrate the tithe (10%) that is set apart for the Lord, then God's covering on the 90% will produce more than the 100% ever could without God's covering.

Many people think that tithing will bring the increase to their lives but this is not scriptural. God's word never promised that he would increase us for being obedient. Your obedience keeps you in position to receive his blessing. Your disobedience exposes you to the curse. When you tithe, you will have enough to meet your cost of living expenses and maybe a little extra. The real increase is placed on the offering. It is with the offering that God places the increase: As you sow generously, you will reap generously. When you give, it shall be given pressed down shaken together, running over. The offering places you in control. I like to say it this way: "When you take care of God's business, then God takes care of your business."

> **Many people think that tithing will bring the increase to their lives but this is not scriptural.**

Remember you can never match God in giving because he gave his only begotten son for us, when we were still sinning and far away from him. He sent Jesus to pay our sin debt (to die for us)! The truth is we weren't even born yet, that's how much God loved us and gave for us. So it is not about matching God like a 401k but it is about obeying God and learning his financial plan.

CHAPTER 15

The Effects of Not Having a Good Money Management Plan

Not having a good MMP can affect us in many different ways. Too often, like overeating, we form bad habits and rationalize our acceptance of them. Most of these effects can be corrected with minor changes in our lives. Let's examine a few of the negative habits that affect us in this area.

Living from paycheck to paycheck, never knowing how much money you actually need. When living with this attitude, that there is just too much month at the end of the money. We never take time to sit down and look at how much our monthly expenses are compared to how much income we have coming in every month. I am not talking about how much you gross in your paycheck each pay period. I am talking about your net amount. That is the amount that you have to spend after all of the deductions have been processed.

What happens if you draw water out of a well faster than you have water coming into the well? I'll let you do the math! The Bible says, "He who loves pleasure will become poor; whoever loves wine and oil will never be rich." (Proverbs 21:17) This means that you can't spend your youthful days partying and buying luxury cars, expensive clothing and jewelry and taking exotic vacations and then expect to have a large nest egg for your children's college fund or your retirement plan.

In the beginning you can't have money and things too. That is a recipe for financial ruin. In our society today, we have too many young adults who are trying to have it all. They are following the life of the baby boomers, they want to start out in life having what it took their parents twenty-years to obtain. They want the four-bedroom house with the two-car garage and the manicured yard. They want the job that pays them more than what their parents are making and if they can't have this, they will go back home.

We play Russian roulette with our finances by getting equity loans and credit cards and other types of loans to boost our spending power. Then when these funds have been maxed out we just keep going from day to day, wondering when our finances will collapse. Will it be a bankruptcy, repossession, foreclosure or, your marriage?

Then we begin to deceive ourselves by saying "It will be better next week." No, it will not. Why would it be better next week when you continue to do the same thing? There is an old adage that says, "Stupid is doing the same thing and expecting different results." It'll get better when you get your raise or bonus: No, it won't. You will just let that money go down the same black hole that the other money disappeared into. Think it'll get better when you hit the lottery? Do you know the percentage of lottery winners that have won millions of dollars and ended up broke? Without a MMP, your lottery winnings will go out of the same door with the rest of your money.

I'm sorry! I forgot that you are a Christian and you don't play the lottery: But shouting out B9 at Bingo is ok? When was the last time you called Deal or No Deal for your Lucky Case at ninety-nine cents a call or text message?

You'll get a part-time job. Why? To have more money you can mismanage? Did you know that most people work part-time jobs to earn money to give away to someone else? I know that your brain is probably going tilt, tilt, tilt! Think about it: Most people work part-time to earn an average of an extra hundred dollars a week. If you take a family of four out to a dinner once a week, you will spend half of what you earned. Not to mention the time you have taken away from your family to earn the money you have spent.

I love to ask people when was the last time they had a family vacation? Most people's response is they can't afford to go on vacation. Then I ask them to consider this: If they spend $5 a day for lunch (maybe more), and don't forget that coffee and doughnut or McDonalds in the morning that is another $5. Now they are spending about $10 a day. That is about $50 a week, $200 a month and $2,400 a year. No wonder you haven't taken a vacation. **According to the above statistics, you just ate it!**

Here is one I know you will recognize. I ask people why they have a credit card. The most common response is that they only use it for emergencies. Can someone please tell me when did Red Lobster or The Olive Garden become an emergency? How many times during the year do you have a repair bill that was over$500? If you were to keep $500 in a savings account, then you could handle most of your emergencies without charging them and having to pay interest. The Bible says, "Of what use is money in the hand of a fool, since he has no desire to get wisdom?" (Proverbs 17:16)

How about this one: "One of these days I am going to start a budget." Hello? Your youngest child is graduating from high school. The Bible says, "All hard work brings a profit, but mere talk leads only to poverty." (Proverbs 14:21) We all know the *I'm Going To* boys or *I'm Going To* girls. These are the people who are always going to do something: go back to school, start a business, write a book, join the church or travel the world. But it never happens. However, they are going to!

Having money without wisdom is a very dangerous place to be. Money without wisdom has destroyed many lives. We see people constantly portrayed in the media that have had their lives ruined because of bad choices. How many athletes, entertainers, movie stars, lottery winners and inheritors of great wealth have we seen end up with their lives in shambles? Money provides many choices. When you have choices and don't have wisdom, it's a very dangerous position to be in.

One day, my wife and I decided to go to the movies on a Tuesday night. When we got inside of the theater, there were only two other people in the entire theater. The movie was about to begin and we were having a very difficult time deciding where we wanted to sit. You would think that should have been the easiest decision in the world for us to make. The problem was that we had too many choices.

When you have choices and don't have wisdom, it's a very dangerous position to be in.

The easy decision comes when you walk into a movie that has only two seats available. Now the choice is made for you. That's why 80% of the people fight over 20% of the wealth and 20% of the people enjoy 80% of the wealth. The more good choices you can make, the greater your value. The Bible says, "Blessed is the man who finds wisdom, the man who gains understanding, for she is more profitable than silver and yields better returns than gold. She is more precious than rubies; nothing you desire can compare with her. Long life is in her right hand; in her left hand are riches and honor. Her ways are pleasant ways, and all her paths are peace." (Proverbs 3:13–17).

80% of the people fight over 20% of the wealth and 20% of the people enjoy 80% of the wealth.

Many people think that having wealth will solve all of their problems. **I know that you won't admit it, but you think it.** Many Christians will say I don't want a lot of money. Then why is the line for financial blessing and restoration longer than any other line at the Altar? I am not saying that it is wrong to be in the line for financial blessing and restoration, as long as you understand that **God is our source. The Holy Spirit is our administrator and wisdom is our accountant.**

Many years ago, I read a book titled Success, The Glenn Bland Method. The book was very instrumental in changing my life. Before reading the book, I had never really heard anyone talk about goals and written plans. Most of the adults I knew were in the survival mode. They would often say, "If you have clothes on your back, shoes on your feet, food on your table and a roof over your head, then you are doing all right." You are successful.

When you are in Egypt (slavery) with a slave mentality, then survival is success. In order to cross the Jordan into the promise land, then you have to take off the slave clothes (slave mentality) and see yourself as a free man or woman. That's why we need to renew our minds when we give our lives to Jesus (Romans 12.2). When we think that success is based on position, prestige and power (in other words, money) **then we are still living in Egypt with a slave mentality.**

In the book **The Glenn Bland Method**, I read about a meeting that took place in Chicago, in 1923 with nine of the world's most successful men in attendance. These men would have been considered in a category with Bill Gates and Warren Buffet today. These men were very wealthy and could buy whatever they desired. Here are their names:

1. Charles Schwab, the president of the largest steel company.

2. Samuel Insull, the president of the largest electric utility company.

3. Howard Hopson, the president of the largest gas company.

4. Arthur Cutten, the greatest wheat speculator.

5. Richard Whitney, the president of the New York Stock Exchange.

6. Albert Fall, the Secretary of the Interior, in President Harding's Cabinet.

7. Jessie Livermore, the greatest "bear" on Wall Street

8. Ivar Kreuger, head of the world's greatest monopoly.

9. Leon Fraser, president of the Bank of International Settlements.

This sounds like the Who's Who for the Fortune Five Hundred magazine. How would you like to change positions with any one of these guys? Before you answer that question, let's fast forward to their lives twenty–five years later to 1948:

1. Charles Schwab was forced into bankruptcy and lived the last five years before his death on borrowed money.

2. Samuel Insull not only died in a foreign land, a fugitive from justice, but was penniless.

3. Howard Hopson was insane.

4. Arthur Cutten became insolvent and had died abroad.

5. Richard Whitney had just been released from Sing, Sing prison

6. Albert Fall had been pardoned from prison so he could die at home broke.

7. Jessie Livermore had died from suicide.

8. Ivar Kreuger took his own life.

9. Leon Fraser also committed suicide.

Now do you still want to change places with any of these men? They seem to have had it all. As the old folks use to say, "They had the Midas touch." What happened to these men can happen to anyone. The Bible says, "Whoever loves money never has money enough; whoever loves wealth is never satisfied with his income. This too is meaningless." (Ecclesiastes 5:10) This was written by Solomon, who was the richest man in the world. Solomon warns us that we must have balance in our lives. When we don't have an MMP in place, we will not be able to obtain the balance we need.

Learn to Build our Foundation on the Rock.

Learning to build our foundation on the rock cannot be done without putting Jesus first in our lives. The Bible says, "Therefore everyone who hears these words of mine and puts them into practice is like a wise man who built his house on the rock. The rain came down, the streams rose, and the winds blew and beat against that house; yet it did not fall, because it had its foundation on the rock. But everyone who hears these words of mine and does not put them into practice is like a foolish man who built his house on sand. The rain came down, the streams rose, and the winds blew and beat against that house, and it fell with a great crash." (Matthew 7:24-27)

When we put God first, he will freely give us the things that most people spend much of their lives chasing. It is a hard reality when you spend twenty years or more climbing the ladder of success only to come to the realization that you have your ladder leaning against the wrong building! The Bible says, "Therefore I tell you, do not worry about your life, what you will eat or drink; or about your body, what you will wear. Is not life more important than food, and the body more important than clothes? Look at the birds of the air; they do not sow or reap or store away in barns, and yet your heavenly Father feeds them. Are you not much more valuable than they? Who of you by worrying can add a single hour to his life? And why do you worry about clothes? See how the lilies of the field grow. They do not labor or spin. Yet I tell you that not even Solomon in all his splendor was dressed like one of these. If that is how God clothes the grass of the field, which is here today and tomorrow is thrown into the fire, will he not much more clothe you, O you of little faith? So do not worry, saying, 'What shall we eat?' or 'What shall we drink?' or 'What shall we wear?' For the pagans run after all these things, and your heavenly Father knows that you need them. But seek first his kingdom and his righteousness, and all these things will be given to you as well." (Matthew 6:25-33)

Not having good money management skills hinders us from being good stewards. **Stewardship is essential to walking in financial freedom. It requires discipline.**

CHAPTER 16

Steps to Acquiring a good Money Management Plan (MMP)

The following are basic steps that we can apply towards good (MMP) money management skills:

Don't charge on credit cards.

Take all of your credit cards out of your wallet, place a rubber band around them, and put them in a safe place. However, if you are going out of town you may need to reserve a hotel room or rent a car then carry one major credit card with you. Before you leave on your trip decide approximately how much the rental car and hotel will cost. Then take that amount in traveler's checks - that way when you get your final bill you don't have it charged on the credit card. How many people would not be on the borderline of financial ruin if they did not carry their credits cards around with them? The reason for leaving them at home is because you can't use what you don't have.

Don't consolidate.

It works in theory but the percentage for success is very low. In today's market, many people have taken out equity loans to pay off credit card debt only to find themselves back in credit card debt and owing more. Their monthly payments are less but they are paying for a longer period and they owe much more.

The statistics show that roughly two of three people who take out a debt consolidation loan or equity loan to pay off debt were back in debt within two years. Their $20,000 in credit card debt has now become

$30,000 mortgage debt and they have added another $5,000 in new credit card debt. It's like buying a membership at the local Spa: In the beginning, it works great, but after a few months **the novelty is gone and so is your money.**

Consolidations are not effective because your bad habits have not changed. Some people take out what's called a line of credit. This

Consolidations are not effective because your bad habits have not changed.

is no more than an equity loan that you can use up to a certain amount. When you pay the loan down you can charge on it again until you reach your loan limit. Most people use it as a sophisticated revolving charge card. One big difference, though -when you don't make your required payments, then you're at risk of losing your home.

Today many people are losing their homes all across America because of equity loans and interest-only financing. Many people have been caught in this trap because they were told that they would be able to refinance when the low interest ends in two to five years. The terms were determined by your finance company.

Many people take out these loans because they are encouraged by outside sources to use their equity to become debt–free. They believe that they will take $1,000 a month that they are saving on their mortgage and pay off their debts. They are convinced that when the time comes for the loan to convert, their house would have greatly appreciated in value and they will be able to qualify for a new loan with no problem. They are convinced (by sources I won't mention) that any smart investor can see that this is a great deal. Don't you think a red flag should go up in your mind when someone says **"Become debt free, borrow from me!"**

They forgot the reason why they didn't qualify for a conventional loan. That their debt to income ratio was too high and they couldn't qualify for a low interest rate. Now when their interest-only loan terminates, the same bad habits will disqualify them for a new loan. Then their old loan terminates and they can't afford to pay the high interest rate on a new loan. They find themselves trapped with no way out.

Don't buy impulsively.

Impulsive spending is a very expensive habit. We often spend two or three times more than we would have if, we had prepared in advance. Learn to plan ahead for special occasions such as birthdays, weddings and anniversaries. Take a calendar and mark down every special occasion you can remember at the beginning of the year.

For example, you know the date of your mother's birthday. It has not changed since you were born. If you have been married for more than two years, you know your anniversary date. Wedding invitations are usually sent out more than three to six months in advance (elopements not included). Don't wait until the last day or the last hour to buy a gift.

Don't buy out of guilt!

How many gifts end up in a closet, basement, garage sale or Good Will because the person that gave the gift was more concerned about how it would look than about the person they were buying the gift for? When you don't have a relationship with a person, it is better to give a card then to waste their time and your money.

Plan your meals.

One of the most expensive habits we have is dining out. Many people spend about 25% or more of their income dining out. Many times, we are so busy that we don't take the time to eat at home. After our busy day, we go home, get the kids and head to our favorite restaurant. Isn't it ironic that one reason we don't have time to eat at home is because we are working overtime or working part-time jobs? Then we go and spend more money eating out!

How many people go to their local grocery store to buy food for two weeks than go out to eat? Plan your meals at the beginning of the week for all seven days. Take frozen items out of the freezer the night before. Set a time for everyone to be home for dinner. Let your kids know that if they are not there for dinner, then breakfast is in the morning. You will be amazed just how punctual they will be after missing a meal.

In the age of fast food, obesity has become a major threat to our children's health and future. A home cooked nutritious meal can be considered more valuable than their college fund when our children are fighting medical conditions such as high blood pressure and diabetes. How important is their acceptance to Harvard now? Not to mention what poor nutrition is doing to the adult population. The idea of seeing your children graduate from college is no longer a guarantee because of poor nutritional choices. There is nothing that can ever replace the love that goes into a well-prepared meal by mom or dad. Who loves your family more - you or the fast food industry? You do the math!

What to do when you want to buy something that is not in your MMP.

There is something you want and it's a big-ticket item (one hundred dollars or more). Write it down and then wait for thirty days. Usually the desire will have passed by then. However, if you still want that item then work it into your MMP. Always buy items such as clothing, jewelry, shoes etc. at the end of the month. This will help you to keep your priorities in order. By the end of the month, all of your expenses should have been met on your MMP. All remaining money should be free and clear with no obligations. **This is a great time to reward yourself for a job well done.**

I remember when my wife and I were looking for our first house. We had dinner with our real estate agent. She took us to her favorite restaurant and she began to ask us questions to determine how much house we would be qualified to purchase. During our conversation, she told us a story about a young couple that she had qualified before. She said they were a young couple like my wife and I and they had very good paying jobs. She told them that they had a lot of disposable income and they were doing a good job of disposing of it!

CHAPTER 17
How to Develop a Money Management Plan

Keep records of income and expenses:

Now it's time for us to develop our own money management plan or MMP. You can purchase a simple notebook or home budget book to keep track of your daily expenses. Start by using the small notebook and list all of your cost-of- living expenses: rent, mortgage, heating (electric or gas), utilities, food, etc. Then list other expenses such as phone bills, automobile payments, credit cards, etc. When you have completed the list of all these items, I want you to take a sheet of paper and draw a line down the center of the page.

Identify the difference between wants and necessities:

Now I want you to write at the top of the sheet of paper, *Necessities* in one column and *Wants* in the other. Many people have great difficulty trying to decide their wants from their needs (necessities) because in their life, if they want it, it automatically becomes a necessity. Without the ability to identify the difference between wants and needs, you will constantly be living a life of disappointment, discouragement, and irritability devoid of contentment.

How can one make the distinction between the two? I am glad you asked. Let's say you are going out for lunch and you are hungry. You may need to eat lunch but it doesn't have to be Applebee's. Maybe you like your shirts ironed and starched. You don't have to send them to the cleaners, iron them yourself. I can hear someone saying, "I don't know how to iron." **Learn!**

You may like to watch movies but you don't need to go to the theater. Rent a movie and make your own popcorn. By identifying the difference between needs and wants, you can determine whether you spend your spare time with the people you love or a part-time job. **Remember, most people work part-time jobs to make money they give away.**

Learn to live within your means while working to increase your bottom line:

Most people struggle financially because they have not learned to live within their means. Many people have a difficult time defining what it is to live within their means. I don't want to leave anything to chance, so let me give you my definition: If you only have $20 then you can't spend $21. Got it? When you make purchases on credit cards and you don't have the cash to pay it off when the bill is due then you're living beyond your means.

The fact is that if you can't live on $500 a month then you will not be able to live on $5,000 a month either. I know you're probably thinking, "Give me the five thousand dollars and I will show you," but the truth is, the same bad money management habits you applied with $500 a month will also consume the $5,000 a month.

The $5 tube of lipstick at the Wal-Mart will now become a $25 tube of lipstick from the Lancôme cosmetics counter. The $29 dollar shoes from Payless shoe store will now become $129 pair of shoes from Macy's. The Chinese take-out you would only go to on special occasion has now been replaced by the top Chinese restaurant in the city every weekend.

You have always wanted to reach this financial plateau. Now that you are there, why are you still struggling with finances? The answer is because you have changed your bottom line but your habits remained the same. **Now you're just broke at another level.**

That's why it is so important to renew your mind. The Bible says, "Do not conform any longer to the pattern of this world, but be transformed by the renewing of your mind. Then you will be able to test and approve what God's will is—his good, pleasing and perfect will" (Romans 12:2). You will need to educate and discipline yourself to appreciate delayed gratification (a short-term pain for awesome long-term gain).

You may have to change some of the negative influences in your life. Like your girlfriend who loves to shop till she drops, or the guy who spends hundreds of dollars on the latest video games or the neighbor who attends all the football games and will only buy box seat tickets. **There is nothing wrong with box seats as long as they don't leave you living out of a box.**

Give your tithes and pay yourself, first.

When we give the tithe first, it shows God how much we trust him. We are bringing to God what belongs to him; we place God first in our lives. We can't give the Lord what already belongs to him (we will talk about this more in the next chapter). The Bible says, "I was young and now I am old, yet I have never seen the righteous forsaken or their children begging bread. They are always generous and lend freely; their children will be blessed. Turn from evil and do well; then you will dwell in the land forever. For the LORD loves the just and will not forsake his faithful ones. They will be protected forever, but the offspring of the wicked will be cut off." (Psalms 37:25–28)

"Then you pay yourself." This means to start a savings account. Whenever you get paid, make a deposit into your savings account. Many people have 401k programs that will deduct a percentage of the salary for them, pre-taxed, to be placed into a retirement program. Although a 401k is a good place to start investing your money, I am suggesting that you also place money into a personal savings account. This will help you to develop a habit of saving and managing your own money.

It does not matter how small the amount is when you begin. A dollar will become ten dollars. Ten dollars will become one hundred dollars. One hundred dollars will become one thousand dollars. One thousand dollars will become ten thousand dollars. Ten thousand dollars will become one hundred thousand dollars. What really matters are the

good habits that you will form and the discipline that you will develop by managing you own money.

I remember when my wife and I did not have a dollar that we did not owe to someone else. When we implemented the above process into our life, God began to bless our efforts. The Bible says, "The LORD will send a blessing on your barns and on everything you put your hand to. The LORD your God will bless you in the land he is giving you" (Deuteronomy 28:8). We had recently relocated from Virginia to Washington State, in obedience to what God had instructed us to do. One day I was reflecting on all that had taken place in the last several months. The Holy Spirit reminded me how we had gone from working with hundreds of dollars to hundreds of thousands of dollars.

Another way to save money is to take a container like a jar or coffee can and cut a slot into the top so that when you come home at the end of the day you can place all of your loose change in the container. At the end of the week add it up and deposit it into your savings account. You can also wait until the end of the month to count your change, place half in your savings, and reward yourself with the other half. You will be surprised how much revenue you can create by saving loose change. My son had come home from his first year of college. He said, "Dad, my funds are a little short, can you help me out?" I went to my bedroom and got my container of loose change. I told him to count it, wrap it and take it to the bank and he could have whatever the final count was for spending money. He was very surprised when he added up the rolls to a tune of over $300.

Another source of income is to re-evaluate how much money you spend on coffee, magazines, snacks, etc. Let's take coffee for example, if you buy a latté at $5 per day that equals $25 per week. That equals $100 per month and that equals $1200 per year. This doesn't take into account that doughnut (fat pill) or sandwich you buy to go with your latté. These are just a few simple suggestions, to help you start your savings account. Create a system that will make it fun for you, then you will greatly increase your success rate. God is a rewarder of those who diligently seek him. That's why I believe it is okay to reward yourself when you diligently achieve your goal.

Basic format for paying bills:

1. Tithing

2. Savings

3. Insurance (for security)

4. Housing

5. Food

6. All other things

This format is designed to help you focus on the important things first by keeping your priorities in order. You will find great freedom in knowing that you have managed your money well. No longer feeling hopelessness and frustrated as when your money was managing you.

CHAPTER 18

The Offering - A Place of Increase

I mentioned in the previous chapter that I would explain more about the offering. The offering is based on what we feel in our heart to give to God, in our own way of acknowledging God's authority and his presence in our lives. In the Old Testament, God used the offering to provide for those who served in the Priesthood.

The Bible says, "This is the portion of the offerings made to the LORD by fire that were allotted to Aaron and his sons on the day they were presented to serve the LORD as priests. On the day they were anointed, the LORD commanded that the Israelites give this to them as their regular share for the generations to come. These, then, are the regulations for the burnt offering, the grain offering, the sin offering, the guilt offering, the ordination offering and the fellowship offering, which the LORD gave Moses on Mount Sinai on the day he commanded the Israelites to bring their offerings to the LORD, in the Desert of Sinai." (Leviticus 7:35-38)

Today God still uses the same system to provide for his church, the body of Christ. The tithes and offerings are God's economic system to promote the gospel and to fulfill the Great Commission (Matthew 28:18-20) The Bible says, "Who serves as a soldier at his own expense? Who plants a vineyard and does not eat of its grapes? Who tends a flock and does not drink of the milk? Do I say this merely from a human point of view? Doesn't the Law say the same thing? For it is written in the Law of Moses: "Do not muzzle an ox while it is treading out the grain." Is it about oxen that God is concerned? Surely, he says this for us, doesn't he? Yes, this was written for us, because when the plowman plows and the thresher threshes, they ought to do so in the hope of sharing in the harvest.

If we have sown spiritual seed among you, is it too much if we reap a material harvest from you? If others have this right of support from you, shouldn't we have it all the more? But we did not use this right. On the contrary, we put up with anything rather than hinder the gospel of Christ. Don't you know that those who work in the temple get their food from the temple, and those who serve at the altar share in what is offered on the altar? In the same way, the Lord has commanded that those who preach the gospel should receive their living from the gospel" (1 Corinthians 9:7–14). God has created a system that allows us to have an opportunity to be a part of his plan for all humanity. It has been constructed not only as an act of worship and thanksgiving to our Lord but he also uses it to test our obedience and rewards us accordingly.

Many people think that the offering is an option to the tithe. They say, "Well, I don't have the 10% for the tithe so I will just give an offering instead." It is not an either or system. God said that we rob him of tithes and offerings! It's not one or the other - we are commanded to do both. That's why some people who tithe and don't give offerings are wondering why they are not increasing. Then there are others who are giving offerings and not tithing and wondering why they are not prospering. The answer is because they have not obeyed God's system. **They are doing it their way. Not God's way!**

> Many people think that the offering is an option to the tithe. They say, "Well, I don't have the 10% for the tithe so I will just give an offering instead." It is not an either or system.

What if you wanted to buy another one hundred shares of Microsoft stock to add to your investment portfolio? You wrote the check out to buy the shares, you called your accountant and informed him to purchase the shares but you forgot to send your accountant the check. One week later the Microsoft stock increased five dollars a share. How much did you earn on your one hundred shares? Nothing because you never completed the process. Your check is still lying on your bureau although you had very good intentions they profited you nothing because you violated the process.

Many people do this every week without knowledge of what they are doing (my people perish because of lack of knowledge, Hosea 4:6). As

I said earlier, we have become bucket plunkers, just putting something in the offering plate without first presenting the tithe. We think that because we placed the money in the offering that the Lord accepts it. The Bible says, "He will sit as a refiner and a purifier of silver; He will purify the sons of Levi, And purge them as gold and silver, that they may offer to the LORD an offering in righteousness. Then the offering of Judah and Jerusalem will be pleasant to the LORD, As in the days of old, As in former years" (Malachi 3:3–4 NKJ). The fact that we can present an offering in righteousness implies that we can give an offering in unrighteousness. That simply means that God did not accept what we offered to him as our offering.

What if you loan your car to a friend for a couple of days and two weeks later, your friend has not returned your car? One day you go to your mailbox and find a note from your friend with $50 attached to it. The note says, "This money is for the gas I have used driving your car, thanks." Do you accept the fifty dollars that your friend sent you or would you rather have your car back? The money he sent was unacceptable because you want what belongs to you. You want your car back!

The tithe belongs to the Lord. You can't give him an offering for the gas and you have taken his car (what belongs to God). It is not acceptable. It is an offering in unrighteousness. The Bible says, "The LORD does not change. So you, O descendants of Jacob, are not destroyed. Ever since the time of your forefathers you have turned away from my decrees and have not kept them. Return to me, and I will return to you," says the LORD Almighty. "But you ask, 'How are we to return?' Will a man rob God? Yet you rob me. But you ask, 'How do we rob you?' In tithes and offerings" (Malachi 3:6-8). God has something that belongs to us, but he will not release it until we return to him the tithe and the offering. **Notice what he did not say: "Return the tithe or the offering!"**

Doesn't it make you wonder what could it be that God has for us? I don't know about you, but I want all that God has for me. The Bible says, "Whoever can be trusted with very little can also be trusted with much, and whoever is dishonest with very little will also be dishonest with much. So if you have not been trustworthy in handling worldly wealth, who will trust you with true riches? And if you have not been trustworthy with someone else's property, who will give you property of your own?" (Luke 16:10-12)

I heard Joyce Meyer, say this one day while watching her television program. She said that God told her, "Joyce, as many people that I allow you to help, that's how many people you can hurt." She speaks to millions of people every day by television, radio and satellite. Can you imagine how much damage that could cause? God proved her in the small things, tithes and offerings (of course there are others but I am talking about finances) before he released his anointing on her to minister to millions of people. The Bible says, "When they arrived, they prayed for them that they might receive the Holy Spirit, because the Holy Spirit had not yet come upon any of them; they had simply been baptized into the name of the Lord Jesus. Then Peter and John placed their hands on them, and they received the Holy Spirit. When Simon saw that the Spirit was given at the laying on of the apostles' hands, he offered them money and said, "Give me also this ability so that everyone on whom I lay my hands may receive the Holy Spirit." Peter answered "May your money perish with you, because you thought you could buy the gift of God with money!" (Acts 8:15-20)

It's not about money! Please don't be that small minded. God wants to release to you true riches. It's about God releasing your spiritual inheritance and his anointing so you can fulfill the purpose he created you for. **God wants to give you much more than money. He wants to give you understanding, purpose and destiny. God wants to empower you.**

Everything you need is already here on the earth. God said that he would open up the windows of heaven and pour *Everything you* out a blessing that you don't have room enough to *need is already* receive. (Malachi 3:10) Most people think that *here on the earth.* means that something is getting poured out from heaven to earth. What do most people use windows for? How many times do you pour something out of your window? Not often.

Then what is the main purpose of a window? I want you to go and stand in front of the wall in the room that you are in now. What do you see—a wall, right? Now go stand in front of a window. Now what do you see? If you are looking out into the neighborhood, do you see cars, houses, the pavement or the sky? If you are looking into a yard, do you see grass, maybe flowers, trees or scrubs? Even though you are not in the yard, you can still see all that it contains. **You are standing in one dimension, while looking into another dimension.**

When God opens the windows of heaven, He shows us where to find the things we need and desire in life. There are no cars, houses, careers, husbands or wives etc, coming down from heaven. Everything we need and desire is already here on earth. What we need is the wisdom (vision) from God to show us where to find them.

We all need God to open our hearts and minds, to see his plan and purpose for our lives. We need to seek God's presence in our lives and obtain his vision for our creation. God wants you and I to impact a world filled with anger, hurt and pain, with love, hope and compassion.

Try me in this Says The Lord of Host!